CW00735391

French History

An Enthralling Guide to Major Events and Figures in the Story of France and French Revolution

Free limited time bonus

Stop for a moment. We have a free bonus set up for you. The problem is this: we forget 90% of everything that we read after 7 days. Crazy fact, right? Here's the solution: we've created a printable, 1-page pdf summary for this book that you're reading now. All you have to do to get your free pdf summary is to go to the following website:

https://livetolearn.lpages.co/enthrallinghistory/

Once you do, it will be intuitive. Enjoy, and thank you!

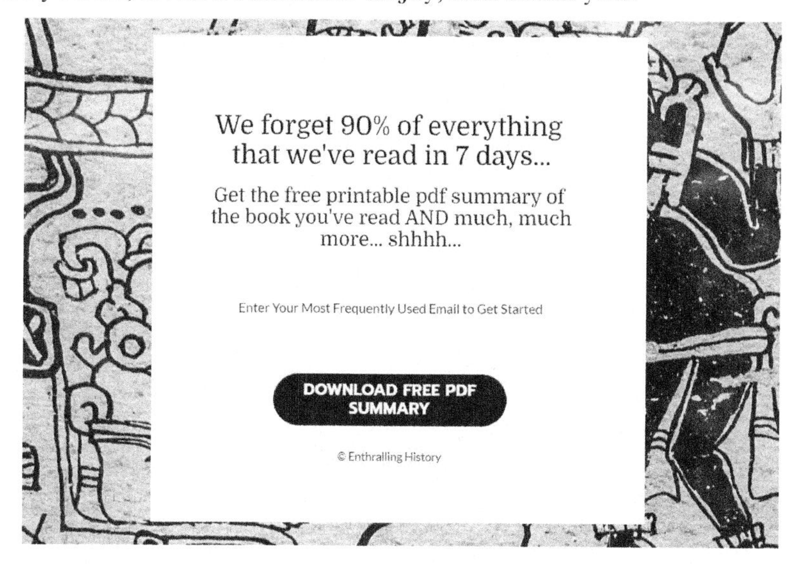

Table of Contents

Part 1: History of France

An Enthralling Overview of Major Events and Figures

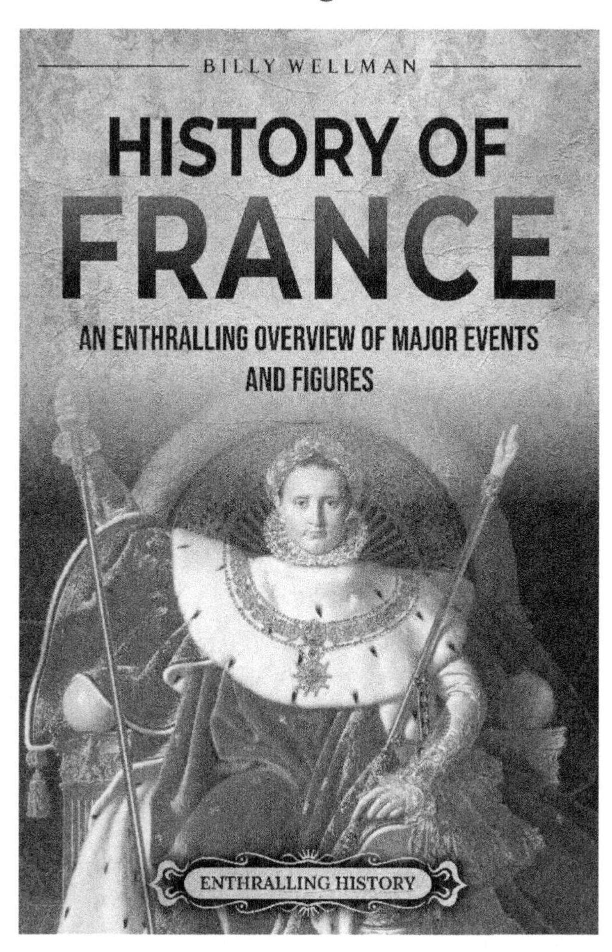

Introduction: France – A Rich Tapestry of History

France has always been a melting pot mixture of people, and its early history included the Celts and Greeks. In fact, the Greeks, fresh from the Mediterranean, founded the city of Marseille in 600 BCE in the reaches of southern France. In the meantime, the Celts began to pour in from the north and would take over much of the rest of what we now know as France, even while the shores of southern France would remain a Mediterranean hub of Romans and Greeks.

The advance of the Celts would only be checked when Julius Caesar took on the dreaded Gaul leader Vercingetorix, coming out on top in 52 BCE. After the province of Roman Gaul was established, many Roman-styled cities were founded, such as Lyon, which would be outfitted with the latest Greco-Roman stylings of theaters, circuses, and public bathhouses.

The locals readily mingled, mixing Celtic and Roman cultures and genealogies. Latin became the dominate language in the meantime, overwriting the more traditional dialects of the region. It was from these Latin roots that the language of French would eventually develop. But as the Roman Empire declined and barbarian Franks and Visigoths besieged Roman Gaul on all sides, Gaul became destined to transform into France, and needless to say, France would go through some rather significant changes along the way.

Today, France benefits from this patchwork, from the Celts of Gaul to Imperial Rome to the Franks to its successive line of kings to the French Revolution and beyond—all of these created the French identity. Even though some of these threads seem as if they are at odds with each other, such as the French kings of old and the revolution that toppled them, both are celebrated for what they had to offer the rich tapestry of France.

For this reason, visitors to France today might just be treated to a commemoration of King Louis XIV (AKA the Sun King), only to witness a raucous celebration of "Bastille Day," which saw the royal monarchy's overthrow. Suffice it to say, France is complex, and its history reflects that fact. In the following chapters, we will unravel all of these unique threads of the French experience and identity as we examine them one by one.

Chapter 1: From Prehistory to the Roman Empire

Even though we do not have a written record from the earliest period of human habitation in France, there are indeed plenty of indications of France's lively, prehistoric past. The rock walls of French caves bear stunning testament to that. For just a brief look into the walled caverns of a site such as the "Lascaux Caves" with its stunning imagery of bulls running across open fields, and one knows that even tens of thousands of years ago, clever, imaginative people called this part of the world home.

It was here that their hopes and dreams were kindled, and their minds sought to explore their surroundings. The paintings found at "Lascaux" are so stunning that some have dubbed it the "Sistine Chapel of Prehistory." Even back in prehistory, before writing was invented, human beings were still just as desperate to tell a good story. And the rock walls of plenty of caves in France were the medium through which these narratives were so painstakingly relayed.

The message that the paintings in Lascaux seem to convey is one of freedom, majesty, and power. This can be felt through the remarkable vistas of powerful horses and bison charging across the terrain. It is believed that the prehistoric French of this period likely subsisted on fish more than anything else, yet in their art, fish was not the focus. The main focus was the animals that were largely unobtainable to them. They likely stared in wonder as these big beasts charged across fields in the distance.

These dynamic animals captured their attention the most, and it was their free and unbridled energy that they wished to leave a permanent testament of their free spirit was an aspiration of their own. Just imagine ancient man hunkered down in a cave, hiding from the elements and potential predators, dreaming of one day being able to charge out onto the open plains of France just like those wild beasts free to run.

One day, ancient man would leave the caves behind entirely and embark upon civilization. Human cities would dot the landscape, and the environment would be mostly bent to the will of humanity.

The Celts were the first known people to make a significant effort at taming the wilderness of prehistoric France. It is said that the Celts, who likely originated from farther inland in Central Europe, arrived in the Paris region and began to use the Seine River near the site of the modern-day French capital.

The Romans who encountered these migrants would refer to them as "Gauli" or "Gauls," Roman words that meant *barbarian.* As such things might imply, the Romans did not look too highly at the Celts of France, and as much as they tried to lump them all together, the Gauls were not a unified force.

The Gauls made up several tribes that often fought against each other, and the Romans often attempted to exploit this fact to their full advantage. Julius Caesar would be the most successful at this, noting that there were three main divisions of Gauls, and he would often play one of these divisions off on the other. Caesar insisted that his eventual invasion of Gaul was primarily a *preemptive* exercise.

He is said to have done this because the Gauls of France often launched raids into northern Italy. When Caesar launched his massive attack on Gaul in 58 BCE, he insisted that it was only to stop the Gauls from launching further raids on Roman territory. As much as some historians may want to write all of this off as political rhetoric on Caesar's part, there is some truth to these assertions. The Roman peace, after all, was only achieved through absolute control of surrounding territories.

The only way Rome could ensure its citizens' safety from Gallic raids was to place Gaul under Rome's control. Much the same thing could be said for the regions of North Africa that Rome later conquered. Until mighty Carthage and other powerful neighbors were subdued, there was always the threat of war. Even worse, the irregular warfare of pirates and raiders could sneak into the Mediterranean and affect Roman citizens as well.

For the Romans, the only way to ensure peace was to dominate and control all of their regional neighbors, and as Roman soldiers marched all around the Mediterranean, eventually turning it into a Roman lake, that is precisely what they did! The invasion and conquest of French Gaul can be said to be one of the first major steps in this process.

There were, of course, great ulterior motives in taking Gaul and establishing Roman garrisons to ensure that there would be no further incursions into Roman lands. Gaul was rich in resources, which would help fuel the expansion of first the Roman Republic and, ultimately, the Roman Empire.

The war against the Gauls also famously benefited Julius Caesar himself. His victories gave him valuable military experience that would serve him well when he later fought to become the supreme leader of the Roman Republic. Every time he returned to Rome in an elaborate triumph (fresh from his latest victories on the western frontier), he was likely preparing himself for the most significant conquest of all: Rome itself.

Fighting in Gaul gave him both political clout and an army that would loyally serve his own interests when it came to that. The clash between the Romans and the Gauls amounted to a titanic clash of civilizations. The Romans had more advanced infrastructure and weaponry, but the Gauls had the numbers and the sheer ferocity (not to mention superb horsemanship) to give the legions of Rome a huge challenge.

Subduing the Gauls would not have been an easy task for anyone, but Julius Caesar was willing to take up the challenge. In these efforts, the main antagonist to rise up against Caesar was the Gaul chieftain: Vercingetorix.

During one of Caesar's first face-offs with Vercingetorix, he lost whole legions of Roman troops to the Gauls. The Gaul leader was not only a fierce fighter and director of fellow warriors but also a long-term strategist who could anticipate the big picture involved in the uphill struggle that the Gauls faced. Vercingetorix knew that the Gauls faced a fighting force with significant advantages; he knew that the Gauls had to maximize any advantages they could claim.

One of the Gauls' primary advantages was that they were fighting on their own home turf. They knew the terrain, and they knew how to best make use of it. Experts at the ambush, they could swoop down on their steeds and catch the Romans entirely off-guard. Vercingetorix was also sure to take advantage of the terrain even when he and his troops faced defeat.

For example, if they were forced to give ground, the departing Gauls were sure to destroy whatever territory they had to give up. They deployed a systematic "scorched earth" policy, which had them setting whole fields ablaze just so the Romans would not be able to benefit from the grain grown there. Vercingetorix only failed in these efforts when he was overruled by several chieftains over the burning of a wealthy Gallic province called Avaricum.

Vercingetorix did not want all this wealth to fall into Caesar's hands, but his fellow commanders could not stomach the thought of destroying it. When the Gauls were forced to depart, the Romans received this unexpected boon to exploit to their full advantage. Ultimately, Caesar was successful, and Vercingetorix was defeated and paraded around during Caesar's subsequent triumph in Rome.

In 52 BCE, the Gauls of France were all but conquered by the Romans. This conquest was not as crushing as one might expect since the Romans were rather inclusive; they were not typically in the business of displacing people but rather doing all they could to *incorporate conquered peoples* into the Roman Empire. And for Gauls, who played the game of the Romans and jumped through all of the hoops that had been set before them, there were indeed advantages in becoming Roman citizens.

By the 1st century, Roman civilization was firmly a part of life in Gaul. No sooner than the Roman way of life was entrenched, it began to be slowly overlaid with something more significant (some would say *much more significant*). In that very century, an itinerant preacher from Galilee, known as Jesus Christ, would usher in a new religion that would take the Roman world by storm.

Jesus lived, died, and, as Christians would tell it, was *resurrected* during the first half of the 1st century. The religion of Christianity was founded and began to flourish in the Mideast shortly after that. It took some time for Christian evangelists to spread this new religion, but thanks to the safety and security of Roman roads, the Gospel ultimately reached all parts of the Roman Empire. And by the dawning of the 2nd century, the people of Gaul were quite familiar with it.

Upon being converted to Christianity, the Gauls could be quite formidable fighters for the faith, as demonstrated by the Bishop of Paris,

Saint Denis, who was martyred around the year 250. Denis and his colleagues are said to have been so effective in preaching the gospel that their frustrated pagan competitors complained to the Roman governor and insisted that he do something about it.

The fact that Saint Denis' martyrdom only came after he was tattled on by local rivals is consistent with how Christian persecution typically occurred in the pre-Christian Roman Empire. Besides specific programs of persecution issued by the likes of Nero and Diocletian, for the most part, most Roman officials operated under a hands-off policy when it came to the Christians.

It was advised to forego seeking them out; instead, it was best to ignore Christians unless specific issues were brought to their attention. As such, it was typically only when neighbors (or, as in Saint Denis case, pagan competitors) called Christians to their attention, that action was taken. The Roman governor likely would have been blissfully ignorant of Saint Denis and his Christian followers unless the locals had not complained about him.

They railed against the Christians as a threat to Gaul's status quo, so the Roman Governor was reluctantly pressured to take action. Even then, a Christian still had plenty of chances to get off the hook. As was famously demonstrated in the account of the martyrdom of Polycarp. During Polycarp's martyrdom, the elder Polycarp was practically begged by the Roman officials to simply proclaim Caesar was God and be done with it, so they could let him go.

The officials did not care so much if Polycarp continued to secretly carry on as a Christian as long as he made a public declaration in solidarity with the emperor so they could send a report back to Rome that they had restored order. Polycarp, of course, was not willing to do any such thing, so he was executed. Much the same could be said for the martyrdom of Saint Denis.

Like Polycarp, Saint Denis refused to retract his faith, and after two years of imprisonment, he was executed. He was led outside of his cell and positioned on a high hill, where a Roman soldier had him kneel before being decapitated. But according to popular legend, this wasn't the end of the story. It is said that the martyred saint picked up the head, stood, and began preaching the gospel again!

It might be a bit hard for us to believe such things today, but nevertheless, the martyrdom of Saint Denis stood out, and the same hill where he met his fate was named after him, referred to in France as "Montmartre." This name is believed to be derived from the Latin words "Mons Martyrum" which translates as "Martyrs' Mountain."

The Christians of Gaul would not have to wait long for their deliverance. In 313, due to a special edict made in Milan by joint emperors Constantine and Licinius, it was deemed that the Christian religion would receive official tolerance throughout the Empire. This meant that the Christians of Gaul no longer had to fear getting on the wrong side of their pagan neighbors.

Yes, now Christian Gauls could accidentally prune their pagan neighbor's tree in peace without fear of the grumpy neighbors reporting them to Roman authorities out of sheer spite. Now they could breathe. And after Constantine became the sole authority of the Roman Empire, he saw to it that Christianity was not just tolerated but became the driving force of the empire itself.

In the meantime, Gallic France would become a magnificent hub of culture and Christianity. Even so, the Roman Empire was well past its prime, and by the dawning of the 5th century, the frontier regions were under constant assault by various warring tribes. The primary antagonists were the Germanic tribal groups of the Ostrogoths, Visigoths, and Vandals.

Of these, the Vandals stand out the most to the modern eye since the words "vandal" and "vandalize" used in common parlance today derive from the Vandals themselves. The Vandals were quite good at conducting sudden raids, and ambushes, in which they smashed windows, burned buildings, and generally destroyed everything in their path. In other words, they totally *vandalized* the place!

But even so, the Vandals actually became the friendliest of these invaders to Rome. Most of the Vandals had become Christians by this time, although their brand of Christianity differed from the Catholic faith espoused by Rome. The Vandals had come into contact with a different variation of the belief system rejected by the Catholics; they followed the teachings of Arius.

Arius believed that Jesus was not equal and one with God through the Trinity, contrary to what Catholics believe. Instead, Arius insisted that Jesus was created by Father God and therefore was secondary to him. Those who followed this faith variant were called Arians and technically considered heretics by the Roman Catholic Church.

So even though the Vandals had some things in common with Rome, the differences they harbored were still more than capable of driving a wedge between the two civilizations. Even so, the Vandals were looked upon more favorably than a group like the Huns, who hailed from Mongolia, whose customs and way of life appeared much more alien to the Romans than the Vandals.

It was Atilla the Hun whose armies would pose a dire threat to the Romans in the 450s. Atilla and his horde would ultimately be put down, primarily thanks to Roman auxiliary units composed of Vandals. It was after the Huns were put down, however, that the Vandals and other tribes would begin to take the Roman Empire over outright.

It was in 476 CE that the last Roman emperor, Romulus Augustus, was forced to step down. Although this is often referred to as the fall of the Roman Empire, only the Western Roman Empire fell. The Eastern, Greek-speaking half of the empire would live on. Even though Rome had fallen, the people of the Eastern Roman Empire considered themselves still part of *the* Roman Empire. Eventually, this half of the empire became known as the Byzantine Empire to help distinguish it from the Western Roman Empire.

However, there would be no return to the Roman fold as it pertains to Gaul.

Chapter 2: After the Fall of Rome

The Gauls were on their own after the fall of the Roman Empire. And in the power vacuum, various warlords, chieftains, and rulers would rise to prominence in various enclaves of Gaul. An early example of this leadership is the Frankish King Clovis. Becoming king of the Franks in 481, Clovis is often dubbed as France's very first true king

Clovis was a force to be reckoned with, seeing that he united almost all of what today constitutes modern-day France under his rule. At the time of his death in 513, it is said that much of the boundaries we know of as France, with the addition of modern-day Belgium, were under Clovis' thumb. Although Clovis is often seen as part of the process of toppling Roman rule, he was also a continuation of it in many ways.

He and his father, Childeric, had deep ties to the Roman military and political machine. In fact, Childeric was one of the leading generals of the Roman/Germanic army that successfully put down the threat of Atilla the Hun. Clovis likely would have continued joint participation with the Romans if it was not abundantly clear that the Roman Empire was in shambles.

Instead of holding up a falling house, Clovis decided to participate in its demolition. In this capacity, he took on a remnant of Roman and Gallic forces in 486, soundly defeating them at the Battle of Soissons. But they were not the only ones he defeated; he also crushed an army of Visigoths at Vouille around 507. A few years later, in 511, he had a city called Paris reconfigured to become the capital of his realm.

Clovis maintained much of the local Roman administration and customs throughout all of this. Although Clovis had defeated Roman soldiers in battle, he still understood the inherent value of Roman civil infrastructure and wished to keep much of it intact. Like many after him, Clovis considered himself not so much a usurper but somehow a continuation of the mighty Rome that he had toppled. Along with keeping Roman customs and civil bureaucracy, King Clovis also adopted the Roman Catholic faith of Christianity. It was in 496 that Clovis supposedly had a dramatic conversion to the faith. He was locked in battle against a barbarian army when it seemed his forces were about to come out on the losing end. In his desperation, he cried out to the Christian God of his wife, "Clotilda."

King Clovis' wife was already a Roman Catholic and had apparently been pestering Clovis to convert. According to Clovis, in the middle of this battle, he earnestly tried his wife's faith; it is said that he cried out to God, and suddenly the battle turned in his favor. He and his troops were victorious!

His conversion was a big deal since, as king, he had his subjects convert as well. This ensured that France, no matter the fate of the Roman Empire, would remain Roman Catholic. Clovis established a long line of rule in what has been dubbed the reign of the "Merovingian" kings. It is said that there were 27 of these so-called Merovingians leading all the way up to Childeric III, the last of the Merovingian line.

Childeric III was superseded by Pepin the Short, which marked the Carolingians' start. The Carolingians would rise to fame with the epic Carolingian monarch, Charlemagne the Great. A few names stand out between these dynastic lines, such as Dagobert I and Charles Martel. These leaders were known for either seizing land in new conquest or for their formidable defense and consolidation of what they already controlled.

Dagobert I is known for seizing Alsace, Vosges, and the Ardennes. The mighty Charles Martel was known for his staunch defense of the realm, especially after the rise of Islam when Martel prevented an invasion of Islamic armies. Even though Spain was overrun and captured, initiating a centuries-long Reconquista to take it back, France under Martel would be the speed bump that would slow down and ultimately stop the Islamic advance.

But who was Charles Martel? He was the illegitimate son of Pepin II, who, although not king in his own right, was a powerful count in the Merovingian kingdom, ruling his own corner of France. He was instrumental in saving the kingdom in 687 and restoring Merovingian rule that had been temporarily disrupted. Pepin II perished in 714, and when France was later beset with strife, it was to his son, Charles Martel, that France looked for its security.

Martel was a skilled and able military commander. First, he took on invading Germanic tribes in the north before sending his troops south to stop Islamic incursions that had spilled out of neighboring Spain. He was instrumental in halting the invaders at Poitiers in the year 732. Although this event occurred a few centuries before the start of the Crusades, the high praise and esteem Martel was given not just in France but all throughout the Christian world was similar to how the Crusaders would be viewed.

Martel was viewed as not just a skilled warrior who had halted an invasion but as nothing short of a champion of God who had prevented the destruction of Christianity itself. It was quite clear that the brilliant Carolingian dynasty of Charles Martel was destined to outshine the Merovingian dynasty, whose fading sun had already begun to set. But the Carolingians were not going to topple their predecessors, as was done with the Romans.

On the contrary, the Carolingians initially tried to prop the failing Merovingians up and only superseded them when there was not much of any other choice. After Martel's death in 737, his sons Carloman and Pepin III worked hard to suppress revolts in the kingdom and take on outside threats, even while propping up the final Merovingian king, Childeric III. For the time being, they were quite content to wield their military might behind the façade of Childeric III.

It was only in 747, when this situation was no longer tenable, that Pepin III (otherwise known as Pepin the Short) became the first Carolingian king of France. His brother Carloman returned to an abbey in Monte Cassino, Italy, ceding all power to his little but mighty brother, Pepin the Short. Pepin was a grand strategist who set the stage for what would come.

Pepin was the first to establish the practice of creating an assembly of nobles to actually "vote" for him to become king. He was also the first to seek out and receive the official backing of the pope. Pepin, in return, repaid the pope's kindness by granting him land in Central Italy that had just been taken from Pepin's enemies; this land would ultimately become the Papal States.

Pope Stephen II officially gave his blessing to the Carolingian crown in 751. Some historians have noted that this is also quite important for the later French kings since this was when the notion of absolutist rule by "divine right" was first developed. After Pepin's demise in 768, his son, the great Charlemagne, became his successor.

Charlemagne would continue the legacy of combining martial and military might with the strength of a unified Catholic faith. In many ways, Charlemagne would kickstart precursors to both the Crusades and the Inquisition in the way he handled the pagan, Germanic tribes in his northern frontiers. For it was Charlemagne that ruthlessly charged into Saxony and took on the pagan Norse, not only waging war against their armies but against their religion itself.

During this conflict, he ordered the destruction of pagan shrines, most infamously, the Irminsul in modern-day Denmark. According to the Norse religion, the Irminsul was a sacred tree or pillar representing the tree of life. It was said among the Norse that if Irminsul ever fell, Ragnarök (the Norse version of Armageddon) would begin.

So, when Charlemagne had this thing burned down to the ground, it probably is not a coincidence that the Viking raids out of Scandinavia that would shake Europe to its core began shortly thereafter. The Vikings apparently felt that they were waging a holy war of their own against the Christian King Charlemagne, and the destruction of Irminsul likely had a hand in triggering it.

At any rate, Charlemagne ultimately succeeded in overrunning Saxony, and that was when his version of the Inquisition began. It was not enough for him to have his conquered subjects pay lip service to Christianity; they had to prove their faith. And if inquiries were made, and one was not deemed to be Christian enough, Charlemagne was not above having them executed.

As mentioned, it could be argued that such things set part of the precedent and the groundwork for both the later Crusades and the Inquisition. At any rate, Charlemagne's greatest boon as it pertained to shaping the dynamic between church and state came in the year 800, when Pope Leo III, beset with his own problems, decided to crown Charlemagne as emperor.

Pope Leo III certainly appreciated Charlemagne's efforts of both spreading and protecting the Christian faith, and he was in dire need of Charlemagne's protection. Pope Leo III was nearly killed by an angry mob just before he crowned Charlemagne. Ever since the fall of the Roman Empire, the Roman Catholic Church had been in a precarious position.

No longer ensured protection by Romans, the pope had to often play local power players against each other in a never-ending Machiavellian bid to stay afloat. However, not all of the popes were always successful in these machinations, and after Pope Leo III ran afoul of a sect of cardinals who had the backing of an aggressive warlord, Pope Leo himself was in danger. He was traveling down the streets of Rome when he was nearly assaulted.

The only thing that saved him was that some of Charlemagne's troops happened to be present, coming to the rescue at the last minute in what must have seemed like a miracle. Pope Leo III cannily realizing who had his back, decided to throw in his lot with Charlemagne entirely, declaring him emperor. No Western ruler had been declared as such since the fall of the western half of the Roman Empire.

In the meantime, the Byzantine successors of the Eastern Roman Empire were quite incensed and criticized Leo to no end. But any threats from the Byzantines at this point were empty and worthless. The Byzantines in faraway Greece were not in any position to defend the pope, let alone attack him. So, Pope Leo III threw in his lot with Charlemagne. This would be the start of what would ultimately become known as the *Holy Roman Empire.*

It is surprising how little many know about the Holy Roman Empire, but this conglomerate of Western and Central European states would become a significant player in world affairs until its ultimate dissolution in the early 1800s. At any rate, this was a big deal, and besides realigning papal authority with Western power, the shockwaves of Pope Leo's backing of Charlemagne also put the first cracks in the façade that Western and Eastern Christianity were united in a universal "Catholic" faith.

The Eastern Christians would begin to view themselves as orthodox originalists and the Catholics as usurpers; the strain that started with the crowning of Charlemagne would continue until the official schism of 1054 separated the Eastern and Western churches for good. At any rate, Charlemagne was a force to be reckoned with. By his passing in 814, he had managed to subdue roughly all of modern-day France and what now constitutes Germany and much of northern Italy.

Charlemagne controlled the largest territory in Western Europe since the days of the Western Roman Empire, so to call him an emperor was no stretch of the imagination. The biggest issue after his passing was how to hold onto and consolidate all of Charlemagne's gains. Fortunately for his successors, Charlemagne had laid out much of the groundwork himself.

Before his demise, Charlemagne took an active role in administration. He traveled widely to install and instruct local administrators and, perhaps more importantly, created a council of nobility that would regularly meet to discuss how best to administer their sections of the empire. Charlemagne is also credited with boosting the intelligentsia of his realm by funding the building of monasteries and encouraging them to become workshops of literacy, in which ancient manuscripts were transcribed and new ones were composed.

It is said that during this period, Charlemagne's monks developed the system of upper- and lower-case letters for the Latin alphabet, as we know them today. It was with the official script's retooling that the region's spoken dialect began to be refined as well. Around this time, the so-called "Old French" first came into vogue. For all of his significant gains, at Charlemagne's death in 814, the economy faced a downturn, and the large amount of land inherited by his successor, Louis the Pious, proved far too unwieldy for him to control on his own.

As such, in 817, he determined to divide his spoils among his three sons. Louis meant for the land to be divvied up after his death, but the fighting over the territory began while he was still alive! In this dynastic struggle, the sons turned against their father and ultimately turned against each other as they battled it out for supremacy. The strife only ended with the Treaty of Verdun in the year 843.

This treaty officially divided the empire between the three heirs of Louis. Louis' son "Charles the Bald" received the territory then known as "West Francia," which constituted much of what we now refer to as modern-day "France." In the meantime, Charles the Bald's brother Louis was given control of "East Francia," which consisted of much of what would later become modern-day Germany.

Lothair (the other brother) was ceded what was then called Lotharingia, a narrow but long stretch of territory that ran directly between West and

East Francia. Lotharingia is perhaps the most fascinating kingdom that came into being since it ran from Belgium and the Netherlands to its northernmost extent; then, as it advanced south, it cut through parts of eastern France and western Germany, as it stretched on past the Alps and into northern Italy. All these things set the stage for the new kingdom of France that was about to form.

Chapter 3: A New Kingdom

It was no sooner than the dust had settled over the Treaty of Verdun in 843 that the successor state of the former Carolingian empire—West Francia—was subjected to several incursions by outside antagonists. Throughout much of the 9th and 10th centuries, the region would face several invasions from far and wide. Islamic armies, Viking raiders, and Hungarian warriors would all test their metal against the blades of the French.

But out of all these threats, it was always the Vikings (or, as they were often referred to the "Northmen" or "Norsemen") who would pose the greatest threat. Ever since Charlemagne stirred up the hornet's nest of the Norse people in the upper reaches of Scandinavia, swarms of Vikings had descended from the North. And whether it was all part of an intentional plan or just happenstance, the descendants of the same Norse people that Charlemagne had insulted would indeed reach the former heart of his empire in West Francia.

All throughout the 840s, the Norse would wreak havoc, raiding French cities, and in 851, they would sack Paris. The Norse would then make permanent encampments along the lower Seine; this would lead to Charles the Simple, who pragmatically realized the difficulty of his own situation, negotiating a truce with the Viking leader Rollo by granting his Norse warriors a long strip of France's western coast, which after that would be dubbed *Normandy*.

The name is derived from the Latin *Northmanni*, which translates into English as simply "Northmen." As much of a blow as this might have been to French esteem, Charles the Simple's gamble paid off, and the Norse proved fairly good neighbors. Rollo was made a duke and became a Christian who swore allegiance to the king of France.

Even so, the Carolingian dynasty had already been disrupted. The end came not through war but through a simple vote by an assembly of notables in 888 which had chosen Robert the Strong as their king. This Robertian dynastic line would lead Hugh Capet to become king of France in 987. But although he is now known as a king of France, at the time, he was more likely to call himself "King of the Franks."

What is the difference, one might ask? Although surrounding regions were arguably his vassals, the only land that Hugh Capet directly controlled was a swath of territory surrounding Paris. And the outlying regions were so hostile and unpredictable that it has been said that his venturing into them would have been fraught with difficulty. Things were so bad that some have likened his condition to almost akin to being under house arrest!

French historian and writer John Julius said:

> *"Between Paris and Orleans, he possessed towns and estates extending over four hundred square miles; there were also a couple of small properties near Angers and Chartres. But nowhere else in France was it safe for him to travel; to do so would have been to risk almost certain capture, and though his life might perhaps have been spared he was sure to be held to ransom – quite probably in extremely unpleasant conditions. 'Charlemagne's successor,' remarked a contemporary, 'did not dare leave home.' It was doubtless this uncertainty, this constant feeling of living a lie, that prevented him from ever calling himself King of France; nor indeed did any of his successor do so until Philip Augustus at the end of the twelfth century. 'King of the Franks' – Roi des Francs – was the title with which he was crowned; and King of the Franks he remained."*

Interestingly enough, if this first of the line of Capet was essentially a hostage under house arrest, it is indeed then quite ironic that the last of the Capets, King Louis XVI, who was killed during the French Revolution, also ended his days under house arrest! Toward the end, King Louis XVI tried to leave his palace on a couple of occasions only to be thwarted and turned back. It could therefore be said that it was not safe for a Capet then, nor for a Capet under Hugh Capet's rule either!

Although his kingdom had shrunk considerably, it was Hugh Capet, who was actually a great-grandson of Robert the Strong, who would start the "Capetian Dynasty" that would last all the way until King Louis XVI and Marie Antoinette lost their heads in the French Revolution of the 1790s. Considering how long this dynastic line lasted, it seems that Charles the Simple was not so simple after all, as his gambit actually paid off.

For the Norman invaders, instead of toppling France, they were ultimately absorbed into the larger patchwork of French society. Even so, it would take some time for this absorption to be complete, and in the early phases, there was undoubtedly much potential for the duke of Normandy to go rogue. This most famously occurred in 1066, when the Norman invasion of England was launched.

In the words of W. Scott Haine, a well-known researcher and writer on French history, the king of France "was little more than a spectator" as this spectacular conquest was undertaken by one of his vassals. As has often been somewhat cynically stated, the Middle Ages of Europe could be summed up as "Vassals and Castles." That is to say, it was from this point forward that feudalism reigned supreme.

France's duke of Normandy may have been an outlier in the independence and strength it demonstrated, but in truth, all of France was a patchwork of feudal landlords who, although swearing their allegiance to the king of France, were indeed in direct control of the land they occupied and administered it and the people that lived therein as they saw fit. It was not always the most pleasant of arrangements, and the welfare of citizens entirely hinged on the kindness (or unkindness) of those lording over them.

But the alternative was not any better for the average person of the time. Without the might of a local lord and his armies in place to protect his subject's life and whatever meager possessions they might have had, they would have been entirely on their own. And in these dark and hard times, peasants simply existing of their own accord in some field somewhere would be open to repeated attacks and raids by any armed bandits that just so happened to be passing through.

As such, most accepted the fate of being a vassal to a strong feudal landlord in return for the protection that the strong walls of their castle and the swords of their knights might provide. As simple as it was, this was the basic social compact of the day. However, the periodic warfare between local lords often became too much for the more peaceful-minded to countenance.

Such things led the church to actually step in, in 989 when church councils initiated the so-called "Peace of God" movement in an attempt to bring about the possibility of non-violent mediation to conflict. This movement was revived in 1027 with the "Truce of God" movement. This movement also took the step to declare that there should be no fighting on holy days such as Lent, Advent, Easter, and Sundays.

As well-intentioned as this was, the fact that folks wanted to kill each other (but only put it off because it was Sunday) likely made the cynical even more cynical. The only thing that slowed feudal warfare down was when in the year 1095, a certain French pope named Urban II called for a Crusade against the forces of Islam. Again, the cynical might point out that perhaps the best solution to stop all this infighting of Christians against Christians was to unite them against a common foe.

But as cynical as we might want to be, and Pope Urban II likely did consider such a thing, we cannot forget that the Crusades were much more complicated than that. As convenient as the Crusades might have been for this particular problem, the pope did not randomly attack Islamic forces only to unite feudal Christendom. The pope was answering a call for help from the Christian Byzantines of Constantinople (later conquered and renamed Istanbul), who were being overrun and attacked by Muslim armies.

The call for a Crusade was initially provoked by Muslim aggression against Constantinople, but the pope then sweetened the deal by declaring that the Holy Land of the Levant, which had fallen to Muslim forces in the 7th century, should also be reclaimed. The fact that the Crusades united the previously fickle and fractious feudal Christians can be considered an added benefit of this call to action but not the actual reason behind it.

Nevertheless, the French (or, as they were still often called, the Franks) bore the brunt of this enterprise. The vast bulk of the Crusaders sent were indeed French, and this was particularly true during the First Crusade. The subsequent crusades would then have their numbers bolstered by English and German Crusaders, but the French would always provide a large contingent of manpower. And when the Crusaders managed to rip Jerusalem (along with several other cities) from the Muslims' grasp, they made a French noble, Godfrey of Bouillon, the king of the newly established "Kingdom of Jerusalem."

The fact that the victors of this conflict immediately fell back on the feudal patterns they were used to is a testament to how fundamentally ingrained this form of governance was. They realized that the faraway king of France would not be able to administer Jerusalem, so immediately, they set out to establish their own local potentate to administer the newly conquered realm. Godfrey was not interested in being called "king" since he felt he was unworthy of such a thing.

As such, he was officially referred to as "Defender of the Holy Sepulcher" instead. Even though unofficially, behind the scenes, he was indeed referred to as the king of Jerusalem, whether he liked it or not. The man they chose for this role was only destined to live on for another year before he abruptly perished, instigating a minor crisis, until the nobles found someone else to take up the challenge.

Regarding the Crusades, the Mideast was not the *only* region in which the French launched them. In the early 1200s, when widespread heresy erupted in the southwestern corner of France known as the "Languedoc," French troops were sent in. The *Albigensian Crusade* had begun at the behest of the pope.

This Crusade was waged against a religious sect known as the Cathars, who were essentially a modified version of Christian Gnosticism, which subscribed to the notion of pantheism. Pantheism is the belief that virtually everyone and everything is a manifestation of God. Although many Christians would subscribe to the concept that Jesus Christ was a manifestation of God, the idea that *we all are* a part of that same manifestation would strike most as absurd and indeed heretical.

But this is precisely what the Cathars believed. Even worse, as far as the Catholic Church was concerned, was the Cathar belief in *dualism*, which spoke of the goodness of God being equal to the evilness of Satan. This seemed to be a rather alarming equivocation for Catholics; to them, it was as if the Cathars were preaching that the devil was an equal to the Almighty. It is understandable why the Catholic Church might call such a belief out.

At any rate, the main focal point of this Crusade, which began in earnest in 1208, was in and around the city of Toulouse. It was here that the Cathar variant of Gnosticism absolutely thrived. The pope was serious about stamping out this strain, so much so that he sent his own papal legate, Arnaud Amalric, to oversee the operation. In the correspondence between him and the pope, Amalric gleefully reported the Cathars' destruction and thanked him for eliminating what he termed "pestilential enemies."

Indeed, the Cathars of France were viewed as a deadly plague that needed to be wiped out before their supposedly "heretical beliefs" spread any further. This was considered important enough that a vast contingent of France's best knights was used to crush the Albigensian sect once and for all. The Albigensian Crusade only ended in 1229 through the signing of the Treaty of Paris.

The future French king's (Louis IX's) mom, Blanche of Castille, played a part in arranging the termination of this bloody affair. Twenty years after the Albigensian Crusade had concluded, her son Louis IX led the *Seventh Crusade* all the way to Egypt in 1248. This mission was led by French King Louis IX. Louis IX would later be known as Saint Louis, and there is a reason for this: he was extremely devout and pious—some might even say zealous—about the Christian faith.

Much of Louis IX's enthusiasm for the Crusades can be traced back to a sickness he had contracted. The illness apparently almost spelled the end for the king, and on his sickbed, he supposedly vowed to go on a Crusade if he recovered. He did indeed recover. And as a consequence, he considered the crusade the least he could do for his restored health.

This Seventh Crusade had an entirely different thrust than the First Crusade. Since the days of the First Crusade, the Holy Land had already been all but lost. Jerusalem was lost to the Crusaders in 1187, and by the 1240s, they had what really only amounted to a toe hold on the northwestern corner of the Levant. Considering that it was Jerusalem that the Crusaders so desperately wanted to take back, one might naturally wonder why the Crusaders did not head to Jerusalem outright.

But there was a reason for that: Louis IX was convinced that it would be easier to establish a base in Egypt, march up through the Sinai to Palestine, and then head for Jerusalem from the south. In 1249, the French king's forces landed in Egypt, and Egyptian forces met the French almost immediately. These forces were being directed by the Egyptian commander Fakhr al-Din. Initially, the French were good at overwhelming and pushing the Egyptian general's troops back. And interestingly enough, they were able to then take the Egyptian city of Damietta without a fight since Fakhr al-Din ordered it to be completely evacuated.

But as much as this might have seemed like a win for the French Crusaders, it was actually a part of the longer strategy of Fakhr al-Din. He knew full well that the French would have a tough time holding and maintaining the city, especially once the hot summer season had begun to take hold and resources would be scarce. So it was that the wily Egyptian general figured that he would move his troops further up north along the Nile River to a garrison called "al-Mansurah" to consolidate his strength and allow the Crusading invaders downwind to become weaker.

He was more than content to wait them out and let them perish, even while daring them to come out into the open and confront him and his troops in an open battle that they were sure to lose. In the meantime, the Egyptian sultan, al-Salih, had abruptly perished. This could have been a boon for French morale, but only if they had known that the event had occurred. But once again, bearing testament to just how wise a strategist Fakhr al-Din was, he kept all news of the sultan's passing absolutely quiet while he essentially served as the head of state.

Louis and his knights finally lost their patience waiting it out in Damietta, and on Christmas Day, they marched on up to engage their opponents at al-Mansurah. Both forces now faced each other from opposite banks of the river. They hurled arrows and stones at one another, even with water between them.

This standoff continued for some time, until the spring of 1250 when a narrow part of the river was discovered that could be successfully crossed on horseback. However, their crossing did not go unnoticed, and Louis and his men noticed a small contingent of Egyptian scouts watching them. The Crusaders took off in pursuit, even though not all of their troops had crossed.

Disastrously enough, they chased the small group of spies all the way to al-Mansurah itself. This played exactly into Fakhr al-Din's hands, as he could now battle the Crusaders on his own home turf. The Crusaders were ultimately decimated, and disorderly withdrawal began on April 5th. The Crusaders were seen running down the Nile River's banks as their enemy stabbed and shot arrows into their backs.

But the worst was yet to come, as King Louis IX was taken prisoner in the confusion. This led to a massive amount of money being demanded for the king's return. For this king's ransom, the French had to raid their own Templar Knights' coffers to get the funds to pay the ransom. Louis ultimately returned to France in 1254 a sad, broken, and disappointed man.

Still, he would try again in 1270. This time around, however, the older King Louis barely even made it to Egypt, and he perished shortly after he arrived due to illness. Ironically it was an illness that had him embark upon Egypt in the first place, and it was an illness that terminated his mission. Nevertheless, he was revered by the French for his dedication to the cause of Christianity and was later declared a saint.

For this reason, there are countless cities, such as "St. Louis, Missouri" or bodies of water, such as the "St. Louis River" that bear this French monarch's name. The great Saint Louis was succeeded by King Philip III. Most historians agree that not much of note occurred during his reign. During the much more eventful reign of Philip IV, a terrible conflict with the Catholic Church was launched in 1285.

Philip IV wished to gain the upper hand over the pope regarding who had the final say in matters of Court and country. Philip tried to resurrect Roman law that considered the "king's wish" as "the law's wish." But Pope Boniface VIII quickly pointed out that the pope was technically given authority by God "over all temporal rulers." This led to a strange and hostile struggle between the French church and state that did not exist before. And it only ended when Pope Boniface perished in 1303.

His successor Benedict XI would last roughly a year before he perished on July 7, 1304. He was succeeded by a pope who would be much more pliant to the French king's demands: Pope Clement V. It was in this backdrop of intrigue and uncertainty that the French state and the Roman Catholic Church would play a part in another infamous event: the dissolution of the Knights Templar. For it was in 1307 that this same power-hungry French King, Philip IV, bullied Pope Clement V to work in concert with him to condemn the Knights Templar for heresy.

The Knights leaders were arrested and under torture, forced to admit that they were heretics. The more cynical will note, however, that the king owed the knights quite a bit of money from previous crusading enterprises, and it could very well be that he just did not want to pay the Templars back!

The Templars were officially dissolved in 1312 at his and the pope's orders. Jacques de Molay, the 23rd and last Grandmaster of the Knights Templar, was executed in 1314.

The execution was a horrid affair in which the former Grandmaster of the Order was burned alive. Before he perished, he fully recanted any admission of guilt and instead placed responsibility firmly at the feet of

King Philip and Pope Clement. As if he had been suddenly endowed with the gift of prophecy, the burning Grandmaster is said to have suddenly declared that both the king of France and the pope would die before the year was out.

He then laid out a general curse on France for several generations. Seeing that both King Philip and Pope Clement did indeed die in 1314, the words of the Grandmaster must have been quite chilling to contemplate in retrospect. And the situation for France did not improve with the deaths of these two men; in fact, it got much worse. There was an economic downturn between the years 1315 and 1317.

If Philip thought that looting the coffers of the Templars would help the French economy, he was proved dramatically wrong. The French had to resort to high taxation, which only made the situation worse. In this backdrop of uncertainty and discontent, the Hundred Years' War erupted in 1337. A few years later, France would be hit by the Black Plague, a scourge that would kill off a significant portion of the French population, further exacerbating economic problems due to a lack of skilled workers.

If the Grandmaster did indeed curse France as is claimed, such things are rather convincing of his words' effect. Adding to these problems, France faced a succession crisis after Philip the Fair's death in 1328. The crisis was not immediately apparent since Philip had three children to succeed him; the problem was that his offspring seemed unable to produce heirs of their own.

This resulted in all three children of Philip the Fair ruling consecutively until the last one perished. And shockingly enough, they each died one after the other in the same year! After the last of them died with no heir, the struggle began to figure out who would be king. This led to the selection of Philip De Valois, a nephew of the aforementioned Philip the Fair.

He would rule as Philip VI from 1328 to 1350. This would begin the Valois line, ultimately intersecting with the Capet line. There were problems from the very beginning. First, there was a rival, a strong claimant to the French crown in the form of King Edward III of England. Insecure about his own place, Valois sought to have Edward immediately recognize him. The fact that Edward dithered in doing so only made Philip all the more suspicious.

Edward himself was a young king who came to the throne at the age of 14. However, he did not achieve true power until 1337 at the age of 17. It was incidentally enough, the same year that the Hundred Years' War erupted, for it was when the young and reckless King Edward III was free of his handlers that he suddenly declared himself the rightful heir to France itself. This is what kicked off the Hundred Years' War!

It is a bit of a misnomer to call the Hundred Years' War a war since it was essentially a long series of bitter, bloody, interconnected conflicts rather than a non-stop spate of warfare. At any rate, for the sake of historical clarity, we will refer to this period of aggression between England and France as the "Hundred Years' War." The English launched the first major offensive during this war in the fall of 1339.

At this time, an army of English troops spilled into French territory and laid waste to several villages, with little or no care for the civilian populations they systematically destroyed. It was a bitter contest between the competing monarchs from the beginning. The French king was so incensed that he challenged the English king to hand-to-hand combat.

The matter, apparently, could have been settled right then and there. But to the chagrin and embarrassment of the French, after the strong and strapping English king accepted, the French king had second thoughts and backed out of the deal! In the meantime, the English received an unexpected boon in January of 1349 when the citizens of Flanders suddenly recognized Edward's claim to the crown. So it was that the war continued.

For several years, France seemed to be on the brink of complete disaster. In 1415, the English successfully destroyed the French Cavalry at Agincourt, and many more disasters would follow. In the spring of 1429, the English were on the verge of seizing the city of Orleans and the whole Loire Valley that surrounded it. They were stopped, not by the armies of the French king, but by a peasant force led by a charismatic young woman named "Joan of Arc."

Sadly enough, Joan of Arc was later captured by her enemies and burned at the stake under charges that she was a witch. Nevertheless, this instance of bravery inspired French King Charles VII to create a professional army that could finally stand up to the English. However, he had to develop a tax lobbied at the average citizen to pay the troops. This was initially called the *fouage* tax, French for a "home and hearth" tax.

The name would later change to "*taille*" which is French simply for cutting and dividing, as in cutting and dividing money. But whatever it might have been called, this tax was unpopular and initiated without even so much as consulting with the Estates General. This retooled and better-financed fighting force ultimately drove the English out.

English forces were pushed out of Paris in 1436, and ultimately out of France as a whole, with the official end of hostilities in 1453. In the aftermath of this war and turmoil, the battles that had taken place across France had left much of the nation in ruin. Writer and historian W. Scott Haine even went as far as to liken the rubble-strewn aftermath in much of France as being akin to a Hiroshima-level event.

Considering all of this destruction, France seriously needed to rebuild its infrastructure in the aftermath of the Hundred Years' War. The remodeling of France would cost a pretty penny or, as it were France, a pretty *livre.* And according to historian Roger Price, taxation in France for reconstruction jumped from 2.3 million in 1439 all the way to 5.1 million in 1482.

Both Charles VII, who reigned from 1435 to 1461, and his successor Louis XI, who reigned from 1461 to 1483, would have major rebuilding projects as an essential part of their rule. Along with building *buildings*, there was also a need to build up the civil structure of France.

Because the French government was on the brink of complete collapse during the worst of the conflict, there was a need to revive much of the natural bureaucracy of French governance. It is said that by the early 1500s, some sixteen million French citizens were administered by a bureaucracy that comprised around 4 percent of the entire population of the Kingdom of France.

Chapter 4: Changes and Rising Tensions

As the 1520s dawned, France did its best to keep its head above international waters. It then came as some surprise when shortly into this decade, war erupted between France and Italy in 1521. We must be clear, however, that when we speak of "Italy," we are doing so in a general regional sense. The actual reunification of Italy into the modern-day nation-state that we know today was still a few centuries off.

Regarding France's "Italian War" of the 1520s, we are referring to a conflict that had erupted between France and various Italian-based principalities. The French king overseeing this conflict was Francis I. King Francis was one of France's most spectacular and dynamic kings in many respects. That said, he was also an "accidental king"—at least accidental in that he only rose to the throne because his predecessor, Louis XII, had no natural heirs.

Francis I was a first cousin of King Louis and had suddenly found himself on the throne. He was not expecting it, but rather than him being unprepared, it was more like France itself was unprepared for the fresh energy and ambition that this unexpected dynamo provided. King Francis proved to be a great political and military strategist, and unlike many of his predecessors, he did not take anything for granted.

Francis came to the throne in 1515, and by the time the war with Italy had erupted, he was still in his 20s. However, the conflicts that kicked off the wars fought on the Italian peninsula had begun before he was on the throne. The first major blow between the two parties occurred in 1494 when French King Charles VIII launched an invasion of Naples. This invasion triggered a reaction from Italian allies Spain and the Holy Roman Empire.

Charles was ultimately made to remove his troops, but the experience cemented in his mind, and in the mind of many of his colleagues, the richness that could be explored in the Italian peninsula. The expedition also demonstrated just how fractured the Italian states were. These findings would lead to the French putting out further feelers to see just what they could gain by aggression in Italy.

The fighting occurred at a pivotal time in world history, just after the reformation had erupted. Interestingly enough, between two of the main antagonists in this conflict—Francis I of France and Charles V of the Holy Roman Empire—there would be quite a bit of personal animosity. This stemmed from the fact that both Francis I and Charles V were in the running to be elected Holy Roman emperor after the former emperor, Maximilian, died in 1519.

The Holy Roman Empire always selected its emperors by way of electors scattered throughout the Holy Roman Empire (basically Central Europe), and a claimant had to gain enough of them to be elected emperor. It did not matter if a claimant was already a king (as was the case with Francis I); if elected, he would have had two titles: king of France and Holy Roman emperor.

The Protestant Reformation once again came into play in the election of Charles V as Holy Roman emperor. Pope Leo was banking on Charles V's support to counteract Martin Luther and the German Protestants. Ultimately, this notion would sway Pope Leo toward backing Charles V rather than Francis I. This served to put a wedge between Francis I and Pope Leo. And shortly after Charles V was elected emperor, Francis I began aligning himself with the pope's nemesis: the Venetians.

With these lines drawn, in November of 1521, a papal and imperial-backed army managed to seize Milan. The French then tried to intervene and get Milan back. This led to armed conflict on January 9, 1522, that ended in a route of French forces that April. The following month, the situation worsened for France since England suddenly came out on the side of the papal forces and declared war against France. Spain was soon to follow.

So it was that the lines were drawn with many of Europe's leading powers suddenly moving against France's interests. France was in need of a powerful ally. This led Francis I to do what, for many Christians, must have seemed unthinkable. He sought out the support of the old foe of Christendom, the Islamic juggernaut of the Ottoman Empire.

It must be noted that Francis I was not as devout as his predecessors or many of his *successors*. He viewed the church as helpful as long as it suited his purposes, but he was not at all against aligning himself with non-Christian entities if it served his purpose. And so that is precisely what he did. Whereas his predecessors, who were still committed to the notion of Crusading against Islam, would have likely rolled over in their graves, Francis I went full steam ahead with his grand plan of hooking up with the Ottomans to offset his fellow Christian foes in Europe.

This led him to send a formal diplomatic mission to meet with Suleiman the Magnificent. However, the Ottoman Turks were not quite ready for such an ambitious and stunning arrangement and ultimately declined. They would leave the diplomatic door open, however, and eventually come out on the side of France.

In the meantime, Francis I made constant reassurances to the sultan that although at times he would make statements condemning Islam and the Turks, this was all for show. In reality, he was ready to deal.

A brief cessation of hostilities was achieved through the unexpected diplomatic wrangling of Francis' mom, Louise of Savoy, and Charles V's aunt (who happened to be Louise's sister-in-law), Margaret of Austria. These talks led to what went down in history as "the Ladies Peace," which ended hostilities on July 5, 1529. This treaty would have Francis promising to recognize Charles as being in control of Naples, Milan, as well as Artois and Flanders.

However, this would only be a brief interlude before the conflict would roar to life again. After coming out on the losing end of international conflict, Francis I turned his attention to domestic affairs. Francis was a great patron of the arts and is often considered an enlightened, renaissance-styled ruler. Francis I established a free university in France, the College de France, which would encourage learning of all kinds.

Having that said, it could very well be argued that it was due to the efforts of Francis and his college that France would later become such a hub for intellectuals. And even though there had been conflicts with Italy, he was not hesitant to import Italian intellectuals, thereby creating the powerful cross-pollination of ideas between France and Italy that would enable a full-blown, international renaissance (or intellectual re-birth) to take shape.

But even during this enlightenment, shadows loomed large. Chief among them was France's backroom dealing with the Ottoman Empire. The Ottoman Empire was once again on the march in the spring of 1543 on land and sea. Regarding its sea offensive, the Ottomans had used their vast Mediterranean fleet to attack the shores of Italy and Sicily. This move had Francis' tacit support, but interestingly enough, it was due to Francis' request that the Papal States of Central Italy be spared and that the abode of the pope was kept safe and secure during this onslaught.

The Ottomans were initially in quiet cooperation with the French, but the dialogue would break down when the Turks became frustrated with French inaction. They wished France to join them on a terrific onslaught of Spain, but France dithered. The French ultimately offered a counterproposal, stating that they would rather launch an assault on Nice instead. The Turks did not like this but eventually agreed to the French plans. Thus, the stage was set for the siege of Nice.

The siege was launched in August 1543. To the shock of all Christendom, France was now openly siding with the Ottoman Turks. It was on the 15th of that month that the powerful canons fixed to Turkish naval craft managed to blow open the walls of Nice, and a joint force of French and Ottoman troops spilled out onto the streets of the besieged city. The city's people initially put up quite a fight, but it was useless; the French and Turkish forces overwhelmed them, and by the 22nd, Nice was in their hands.

It is said that terrible looting and pillaging followed, but it is not exactly clear whether it was the French or the Turks who were primarily to blame for these activities. Whatever the case, all of Europe was shocked at the notion that Christians, with the aid of an Islamic army, would wreak such devastation. The French were somewhat shocked by these developments; their anxieties were high when the commander of the Ottoman forces requested that his fleet and troops be allowed to overwinter in Toulon.

This meant that the French would have to be subject to what was essentially a mini-occupation of Turks on their own soil. It has been said that the Turks who were quartered in France were highly disciplined, and their commander made it clear that any Turk engaged in abusive behavior toward the locals would be severely punished. But even so, the average

French citizen had been brought up to fear the Turks as the incarnation of evil itself, so one can only imagine the trepidation they must have had!

It is said that those who could relocated to other parts of France to avoid being in proximity to the Ottomans. But it seems that despite French fears, the Ottoman stay was peaceful. Nevertheless, it proved to be a heavy drain on the French economy since King Francis had to foot the bill for provisioning the guest army that had camped out on his soil. As such, Francis was eager to get the Turks out of France as soon as possible.

Turkish commander Barbarossa, finally getting the hint, had his fleet depart in April 1544. As it turns out, this engagement with the Turks would be Francis' last major international feat. Shortly after that, he grew terribly sick. In 1545, he developed a painful abscess and would linger on, significantly weakened, until March 31, 1547, when he perished at 52.

In the aftermath of Francis I's death, France had found itself adrift. The powerful and charismatic Francis was succeeded by his son Henry II. Henry was more serious about the Christian faith than his father, Francis. Rather than merely playing lip service, it is said that he was more seriously devout. Even so, he continued the strategy of France, linking up with the Ottoman Turks for extra support against the nation's erstwhile enemies in Europe.

Fighting would continue intermittently in and around the Italian peninsula until the Peace of Cateau-Cambresis was signed on April 3, 1559. Just a few months later, on July 1 of that year, Henry himself would abruptly perish during a freak accident during a friendly joust. He was jousting a younger opponent, Gabriel, Comte de Montgomery, when Gabriel's lance broke during an exchange, and a wooden splinter, shot right through Henry's visor, sliced through his eye, and then pierced into the king's brain.

He would perish in terrible pain a week later. It is worth noting that this incident is heralded as bringing the so-called French mystic and prophet, Nostradamus, to fame since he allegedly predicted it. Shortly before the incident, Nostradamus, famous for writing vague musings of all kinds, had written:

> *"The young lion will overcome the older one. On the battlefield in single combat. He will pierce his eyes through a golden cage. Two wounds become one, and he dies a cruel death."*

Yes, on the one hand, you could write Nostradamus' words as nothing more than vague nonsense, but then again, you could find striking similarities between these musings and what actually happened to King Henry. King Henry could be said to be the old lion who was overcome by the younger man (lion) in single combat (a jousting match). And the fact that he was pierced in the eye, right through his visor (golden cage), is unmistakable.

Also, the fact that the splinter first pierced his eye (one wound) and then pierced his brain (two wounds) to create one terrible wound (two wounds become one) is also stunning to contemplate. It is also undoubtedly true that the king, who is said to have died in absolute agony days later, did indeed die a cruel death!

As it pertains to how the immediate history of France was to play out, it was after King Henry II's demise that France would undergo many dynamic and long-lasting changes. After Henry's passing, his son Francis II became king, but this Francis, unlike his robust predecessor, would have a short run of things, abruptly perishing on December 5, 1560.

He was then succeeded by his little brother Charles, who was then dubbed King Charles IX. Since he was so young, his mother, Queen Catherine de Medici, initially ruled in his stead as regent. Young King Charles IX would have a tough time due to plenty of internal discord and religious strife that had erupted in France at this time. The strife would infamously culminate in the Saint Bartholomew's Day Massacre, which erupted in Paris, France, in 1572.

This incident involved a group of French Protestants called "Huguenots" who were slaughtered in the thousands by an armed Catholic contingent. Charles IX would perish at 23 years old in 1574 with no heir. The crown would then ultimately default to Henry III, the third son of the deceased Henry II. Henry III's run would also be brief and troubled, with his own passing arriving in 1589.

The death of Henry III led to the recognition of Henry of Navarre as the new king. King Henry, subsequently dubbed Henry IV, sought to solve the religious problem by appeasing the Protestants, famously leading up to the infamous Edict of Nantes issued on April 13, 1598. Even while tackling the religious problem at home, he oversaw the expansion of French power abroad, particularly in the Americas, during his reign.

Under this king's reign, in 1608, French explorer Samuel de Champlain established the colony that would become Quebec. This allowed somewhat of a release valve to some of France's internal strife since those disenchanted with France now had the option to immigrate to this new French colony overseas. However, Henry IV's reign would end as abruptly as it had begun when he perished by assassination in 1610.

This led to the rise to the throne of the king's then nine-year-old son Louis XIII. Since he was obviously too young to rule independently, he was governed by a regency led by Marie de Medici. The most infamous member of the king's inner circle would be "Cardinal Richelieu," who served as an advisor and prime minister from 1624 to 1642. During this time, Richelieu would play a prominent role in the Thirty Years' War, which erupted in 1618.

The Thirty Years' War began as a battle of Protestantism and Catholicism but then devolved into a contest over who would dominate Europe. The conflict first erupted when the Holy Roman Empire tried to rein in some of its principalities that had turned toward Protestantism, particularly those in Bavaria which had been drifting away since the days of Martin Luther.

The Bavarians revolted, and open conflict ensued. Various sides and factions developed, and soon France was pulled into the fray. Initially, most assumed that Catholic France would join the cause of the Holy Roman Empire and its allies. But due to the insistence of Cardinal Richelieu (who, despite his ranking as a cardinal, was much keener as a political strategist than as a defender of the Catholic faith), the king of France was convinced it would be much more prudent to come out on the side of the Protestants!

Yes, the age-old hostility and fear of the Holy Roman Empire encroaching on French borders trumped religion; France found itself teaming up with the now Protestant England, the Netherlands, Bavaria, and several other Protestant-backed states against the other Catholic powers. The fighting would largely prove inconclusive as all sides hammered away at each other for several years.

Richelieu would perish in 1642 and would be followed in death by Lous XIII himself in 1643. This then led to the rise of King Louis XIV, who was only a child at the time. His regency was led by his mother, Queen Anne, and Richelieu's successor, Cardinal Giulio Mazarin. Mazarin was disliked by many in France, and he was even accused of having an affair with Queen Anne!

Making matters much worse, in 1648, Mazarin announced that the French treasury had been completely drained due to the expense of fighting the Thirty Years' War. He was only the *messenger*, but somehow wrath was aimed at him for simply conveying the message. This was especially the case when Mazarin let it be known that royal officials could not expect to receive any form of payment over the next few years while the treasury was recovering.

Soon a rebellion erupted, and the situation became so bad that Mazarin and the royal entourage had to go into hiding. Soon, negotiations were started, and a compromise with Parliament was reached, allowing the situation to return to normalcy. Mazarin perished in 1661, allowing Louis XIV to take complete control. He would prove to be an able administrator who could center all French governance around his own will.

This feat would have him dubbed the "Sun King" since, as the planets revolve around the sun, so too did the instruments of French governance revolve around Louis XIV. He seemed a natural for the task, and the fact that he would reign for a stunning 72 years indicated that he was a good fit for the job! King Louis was irreplaceably in the system of France at that time, and he knew it.

He was in fact, rather fond of stating "L' Etat, c'est moi!" Yes, imagine King Louis XIV thrusting his thumb into his chest, exclaiming, "The state is me!" Or, as we would better render it in an entirely English translation, "I am the state!"

The first signal that Louis would be an absolutist ruler was when he declared his intention of not having a Prime Minister. Gone were the days of the meddling Richelieu and Mazarin; Louis would heed only his own advice from here on out. The Estates General would not meet under his long reign, and instead of consulting others, Louis would create an elaborate system of patronage. If you genuinely wanted to have an impact on French society, consultation was no longer the means of doing so, but indulging in patronage was.

In this fashion, King Louis is said to have "pacified" the noble elites by subsidizing them, making them entirely dependent upon his benevolence. And for the rest? He kept any other potential malcontents under wraps by creating an elaborate police force to put down any sign of unrest. The first step of this new system of policing began in 1667 when King Louis created the post of lieutenant general of police in Paris.

This chief of police role was then replicated in all French cities. The lieutenant general was tasked with staying on top of keeping the peace in their district, and as soon as unrest emerged, a crackdown against it was immediately forthcoming. It has been said that the first phase of Louis' reign focused on consolidating the domestic front. With this achieved, in 1673, King Louis began to actively look outside France's borders, and much of the rest of his reign would be spent seeking pure and simple conquest.

But as had been the case before, this warfare and strife came at a steep cost. And by the end of the 17th century, France was nearly bankrupt, so much so that King Louis had to establish a new tax in 1701 called the "capitation" or poll tax, which became a routine burden on the French. Further problems, such as crop failures and disease outbreaks, would only worsen matters.

Yes, things were so bad in France that by the time the long-lived King Louis XIV passed on September 1, 1715, instead of being met with sadness, it is said that it was a cause for many average French subjects to celebrate. He was just a few days short of his 77th birthday, and instead of celebrating with a birthday bash, they celebrated the fact that he had passed!

His successor, his great-grandson Louis XV, was just a child, and Louis would prove to be a complicated leader at best and a wrong-headed one at worst. For it was under Louis XV that a series of disastrous wars, such as the War of Austrian Succession, the Seven Years' War, and the French and Indian War, would all result in French defeat and territorial losses, the latter of which would end with France losing virtually all of its territory in the Americas.

Louis XV would then be succeeded by Louis XVI, who, still smarting from his predecessor's losses, would encourage and support the Americans to rebel against France's nemesis Great Britain out of sheer spite and revenge. The ideals of the American Revolution would come back to haunt this absolutist French monarch when the same notions of universal rights, freedom, and democracy would come home to roost in France. But the French Revolution would have nowhere near as happy an outcome as its American counterpart.

Chapter 5: The French Revolution

Upon the eruption of major world events such as the French Revolution, it is easy to immediately focus on the immediate flare-up and miss out on what led to the conflagration. Regarding the French Revolution, it would be a great disservice to neglect mention of the long stream of events that immediately preceded this watershed event.

And in doing so, we must first cast our minds back to the year 1740, when the controversy over the Austrian Succession came into play. International players squabbled over who would get their hands on the Austrian throne after the departure of Emperor Charles VI. His daughter Maria Theresa was a leading contender, supported by powerful international players such as Britain and the Dutch Republic.

However, Prussia and, ultimately, France contested her right to succeed her father. This dispute came to blows with actual physical combat. It is said that Louis XV was primarily directed to get involved by his influential minister Cardinal de Fleury and other notable ministers of his court, who argued that it would be advantageous for France to join up with the Prussians. But it most certainly was not.

France faced major defeats and setbacks. Their small victories were negated upon signing the "Treaty of Aix-la-Chapelle," ending hostilities in 1748. First of all, the main purpose of the war, the contestation of Maria Theresa to be on the throne, proved utterly useless. She was on the throne whether Prussia or France liked it or not. But much worse in the eyes of many French subjects was the fact that their king voluntarily handed over all territorial possessions he had seized during the conflict. The French king insisted he had no use for them, stating he was the "king of France, not a merchant."

Such sentiment is perhaps more understandable today. After all, world powers today are more in the business of keeping the status quo than of world conquest. For example, the United States might have occupied Iraq and Afghanistan for various reasons, but the objective was never to permanently seize these lands to incorporate them into an American empire. But in the 1740s, world powers were indeed in the business of empire-building, and any voluntary handing over of territory was ultimately perceived as a weakness rather than a pragmatic strength.

And that was the general opinion held about King Louis XV, both in and outside France at the time. The notion that French troops had fought and struggled to gain such territory only to hand it back did not sit well with the French people. The average French subject was so dismayed that they even coined a phrase to express their disgust over what they felt was an immense struggle, fought for nothing except perhaps to aid the king of Prussia.

It was out of all of this that a French expression, which basically means that one is in the business of "working for nothing," was coined. The expression was "travailler pour le roi de Prusse." The phrase speaks of how the French had travailed (worked) so hard for the Prussian king (roi de Prusse), only to get nothing in return, and it came to be used in reference to just about any situation that seemed to qualify.

After the Austrian War of Succession ended in 1748, the French people could not help but feel as if they had been cheated. However, the worst was yet to come when the next round of international conflict erupted in 1756 at the start of the so-called "Seven Years' War." In this conflict, France came out on Austria's side and pitted itself against Britain. This destructive conflict would lead to severe setbacks in Europe, but the worst defeats would actually occur in North America, where the conflict became known by another name: the French and Indian War.

The conflict was called such because the French troops in North America had aligned themselves with local Native American tribes. In the minds of the British colonial troops, their main struggle was against the French and their Native American allies; thus, they dubbed it "the French and Indian War." But this was merely an extension of the same Seven Years' War, which had spilled over into the colonies of France and Britain.

France would come out on the losing end, and after the signing of the Peace of Paris in 1763, it lost its North American colonies in Canada to Britain. Voltaire might have once rendered the comic refrain that the king had merely lost "a few acres of snow," but it was much more serious than that. The revenue of the fur trade, which had long bolstered the French economy, was gone. And in its place was surmounting war debt.

And it was about to get worse.

Instead of consolidating the resources that France retained, King Louis XV's successor, King Louis XVI (who came to the throne in 1774), hatched a scheme to get back at the British. The means would be to use the American colonists as auxiliaries and proxies to strike out at the hated British. This dream came to fruition with the eruption of the American Revolution in 1775.

France came out on the side of the Americans, and though the French government could scarcely afford it, it helped to bankroll the American war. Thanks to French support, the Americans were indeed successful in casting off the British, but France found itself in insurmountable debt as a consequence and, once again, with next to nothing to show for it.

Perhaps it pleased the king to get revenge on the British, but the French, struggling to purchase bread and other bare essentials in the marketplace, were none too happy. Were they once again working for the king of Prussia? Or, as it were this time, were the French working for George Washington? And with absolutely nothing to show for it except inflated prices in the marketplace?

At this point, French society had reached a tipping point. The masses' discontent was palpable, and the French intelligentsia was pouring gasoline on the fire, hammering out pamphlet-after-fiery-political-pamphlet decrying the king and the general state of affairs. They also pointed out the ironic fact that the French had supported an American Revolution that threw off the English king, yet the French people were still getting around to the whims of their highly unpopular French king.

King Louis XVI certainly was not a big fan of the ideology of the American Revolution; for him, it was merely a means to an end. However, all of this would come back to bite him in a big way when the same notions of overthrowing the monarchy and establishing the French Republic became the rallying cry of the French masses. This situation was exacerbated because most taxes were being leveled at the poorer classes of French society rather than the more affluent.

Even though the more well-off French subjects often found ways to avoid taxation, the poor were relentlessly targeted with the taille tax, which would continue to be an enormous source of resentment. At this time, France's society was divided into three distinct categories or, as the French termed it, *estates.* There was the First Estate, which comprised the rich, aristocratic class, and the Second Estate, which comprised the Clergy.

Both of these classes often found a way around taxation. It was then the Third Estate, comprised of commoners who typically carried the full brunt of taxation. And all of this without much of any representation. The Estates General, the representative body meant to represent the estates, had not met in several years. It was only after great public outcry that King Louis XVI agreed to have the Estates General meet in February of 1787.

During this meeting, the king ironically heard the same rallying cry that had stirred the Americans to rebel against the king of England for he heard a unanimous shout of "no taxation without representation." King Louis was increasingly alarmed at these developments and attempted to stifle the growing outrage by suspending parliament. This backfired spectacularly when protests left the official chambers of discourse and ended up out in the street. Louis then reluctantly reconvened the Estates General on May 1, 1789.

In the meantime, the printing press of France was in overdrive, pumping out all manner of political pamphlets disparaging the French royal family and blaming them for all of the problems that the average subject of France was facing. One of the most popular pamphlets then was a work by Abbe Emmanuel Sieyes entitled "What is the Third Estate?"

After asking that question, this piece concluded that since it represented the vast bulk of the French people, the Third Estate *was the French people.* The thrust of the discourse was to encourage the French masses to rise up and claim their rights since they, the oppressed majority, were the true embodiment of the French nation. During this period, King Louis XVI seemed to follow a predictable pattern of being cowed by popular opinion, followed by his immediate alarm and attempts to crack down.

The crackdowns would then backfire, the people would be emboldened, and King Louis XVI would be further cowed and bullied. This basic pattern would repeat itself throughout the rest of King Louis XVI's troubled reign. At the outset of the Third Estate's rise to political prominence, King Louis, after calling for the Estates General to meet, grew so alarmed at what was happening that on June 20, 1789, he locked up the meeting hall so the Third Estate could not convene!

Undaunted, the Third Estate met at a public tennis court instead, where they issued their Tennis Court Oath that they would not depart until their demands, most notably a new constitution, would be met. This feat of solidarity and defiance once again cowed the king into submission, and he caved into their demands for a meeting in the National Assembly.

Once they were present at the National Assembly, declarations for establishing a "Constituent Assembly" and signing nothing short of a new constitution were made. The king, backed into a corner, felt no choice but to comply. He immediately regretted his decision and began mobilizing troops around Paris in case things turned ugly.

And turn ugly they did.

On July 14, 1789, French revolutionaries stormed the Bastille, a royal fortress/prison in Paris.

Although the storming of the Bastille is still celebrated in France, it was the start of an explosion of unbridled human emotion that would lead to some rather bloody and monstrous consequences. The storming of the Bastille was mainly done to retrieve weapons and ammunition, although the prisoners who were being kept there were also released. The guards initially held off the crowd, but once the Bastille was on the verge of being overwhelmed, those in charge agreed to hand over the fortress under the promise that their lives would be spared. They were not.

Instead of sparing the lives of those inside as promised, the mob tore them limb from limb. With bloody heads and other body parts being waved in the air by a delighted and bloodthirsty mob, the French Revolution had begun. Adding more fuel to the fire was the fact that bread prices continued to rise in the market. It may seem like a simple thing, but it was not. If prices are so inflated that the average person cannot buy food, local populations will not be content. If the problem is not solved quickly, that discontent can spill over into absolute rage.

And this was indeed what happened in France.

The king was sitting on a powder keg whether he realized it; without proper relief, his subjects were ready to let him know their desperation firsthand. This was most famously demonstrated on October 5, 1789, when a mob (led predominantly by women) marched on the king's palace in Versailles. There, all those desperate mouths desiring bread clamored that they were about to drag out the "baker, the baker's wife, and the baker's son" by force if need be.

The baker reference was a jibe at the king and his family. Sadly, plenty of people among that desperate mob were deluded enough to believe that the capture of the king would solve all of their problems. It was much simpler than that. Grabbing King Louis would certainly not ensure the poor and needy a lifetime supply of bread. But although the poor, deluded masses provided the brawn, the intelligentsia was the brains of this operation.

Several political clubs had sprung into existence. Leading the charge was a club that met in the Convent of the Jacobins, known as "Jacobins." The firebrand political ideologues of the Jacobins led the charge in stirring up the French masses as their own personal attack dogs to use against the French king. Their arguments were both complex and simple at the same time. They spoke of high-flung goals and aspirations yet dumbed things down so much that anyone could understand them when needed.

At the most simplistic level, one could imagine a Jacobin asking a hungry French mob, "You want bread?" before pointing his finger at the French king and shouting, "Well, that is the baker! Go get him!" Even worse than pointing fingers at the French king and urging mobs to attack him when it suited their purpose, the intelligentsia was not above spreading absolute lies.

After a catastrophically failed harvest in 1789, a terrible conspiracy theory known as the "Great Fear" suggested a royal and aristocratic plot in the works to kill off the peasants by deliberately destroying crops. The notion is just as ridiculous as it sounds, but as French historian and writer W. Scott Haine once put it, "in the overheated and undernourished minds of the peasantry," it seemed to work.

Lies were spread to further disparage the king and absolute fury and hatred were stoked in the hearts of the average French subject. King Louis was largely oblivious to what was happening in his kingdom and ultimately became a prisoner. He was marched off to Paris, where the revolutionaries carefully watched him.

Sick of his veritable confinement, the king and his family attempted to slip away in 1791, only to be found out and forced to turn back. From this point forward, there was no mistake; the king and his whole court were under house arrest. An arrest ended with the king's execution on January 21, 1793, and the queen's execution on October 16 of that same year.

But if the average French citizen felt that their suffering would end or that they would have an adequate supply of bread with the killing of the king and queen of France, they were mistaken. On the contrary, the lives of the average person were about to get a lot worse as the intelligentsia that had mobilized the mob began to turn on the mob itself.

When further demonstrations were held attempting to protest the dire state of the French people, the Jacobins, under the agency of the newly established Committee on Public Safety, launched a campaign of sheer terror against them. Now those people in the streets demanding bread, those who had been weaponized by the intelligentsia to use against the royal family, were suddenly dubbed as enemies of the revolution. And no matter how much they protested the inflated, high prices, complaints about bread were no longer palatable to the intelligentsia elites.

The leading architect of the terror, Jacobin giant Maximilian Robespierre, showed his utter disdain and contempt for the poor, starving masses by condemning them for having nothing better to complain about than "paltry merchandise." But in truth, most of the masses just wanted stable bread prices. The intelligentsia desired revolution and used the hungry masses as tools to get it.

The Jacobins got their revolution, but the mobs of distressed citizens they used to obtain it did not get their bread. They had been duped into "working for the king of Prussia" once again. Yet this Jacobin stand-in for the king of Prussia not only tricked them as a means to their ends, but they were also ready to dispatch with them when they no longer served their purpose.

As such, a wave of terror was launched against anyone who dared criticize or question the regime. Soon heads were being chopped off at an astonishing rate, as a climate of absolute paranoia and fear was created. The only thing that ended this terror was when Robespierre himself was executed. In the aftermath, Napoleon Bonaparte, a powerful and charismatic general, came to power.

He ultimately became the dictator of France. Lending yet another layer of irony, the French Revolution that sought to rid France of an absolutist monarch ended by establishing another, for it was in 1802 that Napoleon was made dictator as "Consul for Life." This was followed up with his being given the entirely ostentatious title of "Emperor of France" in 1804. And to add yet more insult to injury, it was declared that all of his offspring would inherit the same title!

Napoleon had just begun a new dynastic line of tyrants. Yes, the French had apparently been struggling for nothing. They had fought for the king of Prussia and gained nothing for their efforts. No bread, no end to the monarchy, nothing for their trouble but Napoleon Bonaparte and a series of protracted warfare that would erupt across Europe and beyond.

Chapter 6: The Napoleonic Wars

Although Napoleon looms large in French history, he was actually a native of Corsica, which was not acquired by France until 1768. Ironically, if France had never taken over the little island of Corsica, it is highly likely that Napoleon Bonaparte would never have become the emperor of France. Perhaps emperor of a small Mediterranean island, but France? Not likely!

Regarding the governance of France itself, Napoleon first came to prominence in the aftermath of the terror when a so-called "Directory" was established to restore order. One of the members of the director was French General Paul Barras. Napoleon was in good with Barras, and through him, he gained increased influence in French governmental affairs. Napoleon had returned to France fresh from foreign battles, only to be called upon by the Directory to put down a revolt deemed "counterrevolutionary."

Napoleon used his soldiers to put down the unrest and was made the "Commander of the Army of the Interior." Napoleon was then given the authority to send his soldiers door-to-door to seize weapons. Ironically enough, all of the weapons pilfered from French garrisons (such as the Bastille) at the outset of the revolution were now being seized and taken from the citizens! With internal unrest stabilized, Napoleon once again led French forces abroad, just in time to take on the latest coalition of international forces that had risen against France.

Napoleon stifled the Italians at Piedmont in the spring of 1796, then marched on Austria, forcing them into a peace treaty on October 17,

1797. This involved the dismantling of the Republic of Venice. Among the many policies that Napoleon shattered, this was one of the longest-lived, stretching back over a thousand years. Yet, Napoleon was able to bully the Venetians into being divided between the French and the Austrians as part of the Treaty of Campo Formio.

With the Austrian and Italian fronts secure, the only bane of Napoleon's existence to remain was that of England. Initially, an amphibious assault on Britain was considered, but it did not take long for Napoleon and his colleagues to realize the impossibility of such a feat. The British had the best navy in the world at the time, and France's tattered naval vessels did not stand much of a chance.

It was in light of all this that Napoleon and company considered an alternative; if they could not put a dent in England by crossing the English Channel, they would instead cross the Mediterranean. Napoleon sent a French fleet to Egypt to take on British interests in the region. Britain was heavily involved in trade here, and it was believed that Egypt could serve as a stepping stone to the crown jewel of the British Empire: India.

With this in mind, the French launched across the Mediterranean to Egypt. Before they landed off the Egyptian coast, however, they first made a pitstop in Malta, where Napoleon saw to it that he ruined and dismantled yet another ancient order, none other than the Knights Hospitaller. The Hospitaller Knights had been holed up in Malta since the Crusades.

Napoleon decided to forcibly disband them and seize their island. He now had Malta as a base of operations right in the middle of the Mediterranean. It was after this that he and his troops headed off to Egypt. This was not the first time in history that a French army had invaded Egypt. The same feat had been attempted by Saint Louis himself during the 7th Crusade. But although the action was being repeated, the motives and cast of characters had significantly changed.

This was by no means a religious crusade. And Napoleon was not a Christian crusader. On the contrary, upon reaching the gates of Alexandria, he had interpreters proclaim to the stunned Egyptians that he respected Mohammad and Islam and was there to free them from the Mameluke warriors that had recently taken control of the nation.

Napoleon had gotten this idea that he could break the Mameluke's hold of Egypt and repatriate Egypt back to the Ottoman Empire, which had since lost much of any real control over the region. Napoleon proclaimed as much, but the locals were either not keen to be returned to the sultan, or they did not care too much for French invaders suddenly dropping down in their backyard.

Either way, the locals were sure to give Napoleon and company as hard a time as they possibly could. And no matter how much he might have stressed that he was "on their side," no one seemed to believe it. Nevertheless, Napoleon successfully seized Alexandria, making it a new forward base of operations. From here, Napoleon's forces would launch an assault on Cairo. The struggle for Cairo would occur on July 21, 1798, and go down in history as the "Battle of the Pyramids."

At this point, Napoleon may have seemed rather ingenious, but there was a coalition of European powers forming against him—the second coalition, to be exact. As it turns out, the Russians were quite miffed over what had happened in Malta. Tsar Paul had been an honorary grand master of the Hospitallers; soon, Russia was getting involved. The War of the Second Coalition would have England and Russia team up against the French. And as much as Napoleon dreamed of becoming the best friend of the Ottomans, they ended up throwing in their lot with the Second Coalition as well.

The forces of the Second Coalition and the French engaged each other in the summer of 1799 as they duked it out in the Netherlands. The French had some Dutch allies on hand as they attempted to repel the coalition forces from Holland. After sustaining heavy casualties, the Coalition force was ultimately forced to flee after the Battle of Castricum on October 6, 1799.

Napoleon had just returned from his misadventure in Egypt (a costly one that saw the French fleet smashed by British Admiral Horatio Nelson) and found France again suffering from internal discord and turmoil. Napoleon, seeking to restore order, used the men under his command to forcibly seize power on November 9, 1799.

He was made First Consul of France, which essentially made him the dictator of the whole nation. Shortly after this rank was achieved, Napoleon engaged Coalition forces on June 14, 1800, at the Battle of Marengo in northern Italy. The Coalition forces were ultimately defeated, and the French gained complete control of Italy.

Napoleon returned to France in triumph, and just a couple of years later, in 1802, he was made Consul for Life. This was then followed by his being hailed as emperor in 1804. That same year, Napoleon rolled out his own civil code (later known as the Napoleonic Code), which codified into law many of the ideals of the Revolution, albeit with the authoritarian force of Napoleon behind them.

This civil code made sure that some semblance of equality was given to French citizens and established a meritocracy in which one could rise through the ranks of French society by virtue of their own particular skills rather than through birth or by merely buying their way into a guild, as had been all too common in the past. Even after Napoleon was long gone, establishing this civil code would be one of his most lasting legacies.

France and Britain had temporarily called a truce due to the signing of the Treaty of Amiens in 1802. This temporary ceasefire had already broken down shortly after Napoleon was crowned emperor in 1804. As beaten and battered as their navy already was, the French began to challenge the British on the high seas as thoughts again turned to the idea of an invasion of Britain.

But once the British smashed the French ships at Cape Finisterre in July of 1805 and trounced the French Navy at Trafalgar a short time later, all plans to invade Britain by sea were shelved. Instead, Napoleon revamped his warfare over land; striking out at the Coalition army assembled at Austerlitz, he dealt the Austrian and Prussian armies a terrible blow that December.

And even though the British were just out of reach, Napoleon embarked upon a strategy of economic warfare. Consolidating his control over the European continent, he sought to exclude the British from all trade by instituting his "Continental System." He hoped he could choke Britain of essential resources, but Britain's robust trade still managed to get through several holes in Napoleon's system.

One of those holes was Russia, which, although not at war with Napoleon, proved to only half-heartedly comply with Napoleon's Continental policy. This led Napoleon to make plans for an invasion of Russia itself. This disastrous invasion was launched in June of 1812. Napoleon had cobbled together a large army of some 600,000 troops at this point, and if he could face off with Russian forces in open combat, he had a good chance of victory.

However, the Russian commanders in the field were smart enough to deprive Napoleon of this opportunity. Instead of facing him in open combat, they carefully withdrew, leading Napoleon further and further into Russia. As the Russian armies departed, they deployed a scorched earth policy, burning everything behind them as they fled. This was done so that Napoleon's conquering armies would find nothing to help sustain them.

They then fought a terrible battle with Russian troops near Moscow. The French were victorious but at the cost of some seventy thousand dead French troops. The Russian army was not defeated; it merely decided to withdraw farther east. Napoleon made it all the way to Moscow, only to find it virtually abandoned and burned to a crisp! As such, he could not supply his troops, and as the harsh Russian winter set in, they were in for a terrible time as the soldiers could barely keep warm and faced the threat of frostbite.

There was also the problem of random attacks by the few citizens who hung around the city. They could trust no one, had no food, and could barely keep warm. To his chagrin, Napoleon realized that although he was occupying the Russian capital, with the Russian army lurking in the far eastern frontier of the nation, he could not say that he had conquered Russia.

Instead, he was forced to flee from his illusory conquest and send his freezing, starving troops on a humiliating and deadly march back to France. As soon as they turned tail and ran, the Russian army came out from hiding in the east and mercilessly harassed the fleeing French soldiers. Tens of thousands of French soldiers lost their lives; many simply froze to death.

It is said that this terrible episode marked the second time that Napoleon abandoned his troops since he hopped on a fast sled back to France while the rest of his army slowly and painfully slogged their way back home on foot. As in Egypt, Napoleon arrived back in Paris to do damage control before word of his terrible defeat became widely known.

It did not matter; the writing was already on the wall. And after another disastrous loss to the coalition at Leipzig in October of 1813, Napoleon knew it was over. He ultimately sued for peace in the spring of 1814 and abdicated on April 4. In the terms of the subsequent agreement, the Treaty of Fontainebleau, France was stripped of its empire, and Napoleon himself was exiled to a tiny island called "Elba" in the middle of the Mediterranean.

Louis XVIII, the brother of the deceased Louis XVI, was placed on the French throne. France seemed to have come full circle; the monarchy that so many heads had rolled over was back in force. But this, of course, was not the end of the story. Napoleon would stage a great escape from his island prison and, for one hundred heady days, would lead France once again.

On February 26, 1815, Napoleon managed to sneak on board a French brig called *L'Inconstant* and land in mainland France on March 1. News of his escape had already gotten out, and a French army was sent to apprehend the fugitive former emperor. But in one of Napoleon's most memorable moments, rather than run from these troops sent to seize him, he ran toward them.

It is said that he opened up his coat and dared the incoming troops to shoot him on the spot. Napoleon supposedly shouted, "If any of you would shoot his Emperor, here I am!" Instead of shooting or even simply arresting the dictator, the troops broke out into spontaneous cheers! Just like that, Napoleon was back in charge of one of Europe's most powerful armies.

In retrospect, it might seem predetermined that Napoleon's troops would celebrate him this way. But if we were to truly consider the mood and atmosphere of France at the time, this gamble that Napoleon made was *far from certain.* Yes, many were indeed upset with the return of the old French monarchy, the loss of empire, and the general feeling of being bullied by other European powers, but at the same time, many among the French were quite frustrated with Napoleon himself.

Some did not hesitate to blame him for France's recent miseries. One of the former French marshals, Michel Ney, had, just before Napoleon's return, gone on the record to state that he felt that Napoleon should be held responsible for many of France's problems and even went as far as to state that Napoleon "should be brought back in an iron cage."

Yet, after Napoleon returned, most began singing a different tune - *literally.* They were singing the song of "Vive l' Empereur!" and there was suddenly hope that Napoleon would somehow reverse the recent misfortunes of France.

But it was not to be.

Foreign powers refused to even recognize Napoleon as a legitimate leader at this point, and on March 25, 1815, yet another coalition of Britain, Russia, Austria, and Prussia came into being to stop Napoleon in his tracks.

This coalition would render Napoleon's final defeat in the Battle of Waterloo, which took place that June. Napoleon was forced to flee back to Paris with what remained of his shattered army. There, he once again stepped down as ruler of France, abdicating on June 22. He attempted to slip away once again as the coalition forces closed in, but he found all of the ports blocked.

Knowing there was nowhere to run and not wanting to be hunted down like a dog, Napoleon decided to turn himself over to the British. Napoleon surrendered on July 15 and was soon on a British ship to head off to his next destination in exile: the island of St. Helena. He would spend his final days here until he perished on May 5, 1821.

Chapter 7: The Long 19th Century

It was only after Napoleon was deposed for good that King Louis XVIII got a firm grip on the French throne. Louis and his regime were initially quite good at balancing the royalist faction in France with the new class of notables that had emerged since the French Revolution. One of the critical architects in this balancing act was the king's minister, Elie Decazes.

The king, while being part of the royal restoration, made sure to abide by a new charter that recognized most of the democratic gains of the revolution. Much of the same promised freedoms that the French Revolution claimed to endorse would also be protected and supported by the French king. His reign would last until 1824, when due to a wide variety of afflictions, including gout and even a bout of gangrene, he perished on September 16 of that year.

This marked the final time in history when a French king would perish while still in power. Upon his passing, the "Comte d' Artois" would be tapped to succeed him as King Charles X. Charles X was another older king; he was already 67 years old when he was crowned. Despite his age, he seemed to lack the wisdom many hoped he might bring to the throne.

Instead, he seemed to be a man stuck in the past. Whereas his predecessor Louis XVIII was keenly aware of the changes that had been made to French society and had sought to adapt and compromise royal protocols to go along with it, Charles seemed as if he wanted to roll back all of the gains of the revolution and return to an absolute monarchy.

The first signal that this was the case came on May 29, 1825, when Charles X was crowned at Reims Cathedral in an elaborate and ostentatious display, which had not occurred since the days of the Ancien Régime. Needless to say, this would not sit well with the French people. Even so, Charles X proved to be quite an adventurist. In much the same way as Napoleon, his exploits overseas served as a great distraction to the problems occurring at home.

For it was in July of 1830 that he directed French forces to engage in an expedition in Algeria. Soon the French flag was flying over Algeria, and the French would occupy this piece of North African real estate for over a century, not officially exiting until 1962. As much of a distraction, as these external developments might have provided, it could not prevent the continuing internal discord from finally showing through.

King Charles X had already made moves to suspend the constitution, and that July, he worked to censor what had previously been a free press. Since the notion of a free press and the rights promised in the constitution were central to the gains of the French Revolution; those against a return of absolutist monarchy were naturally aghast. The question was what was anyone going to do about it.

As for the printing presses, it is said that in one example, after an official showed up with some personnel to dismantle one of them, as soon as he left the scene, those same workers put it right back together in complete defiance of what they had just been ordered to do. Even more ominous for the regime was when a massive group of protesters showed up just outside the Palais-Royal, demanding their rights to be recognized.

With memories of such things as the storming of the Bastille not that far removed from history at this point, it seemed that just about anything could happen. The fears of officials in charge of keeping the peace were also exacerbated by the fact that the best legions of French troops were down in Algeria. Having that said, if there was indeed a major uprising, it would have been difficult to put down.

Making matters even worse, many of the soldiers stationed in France began to defect over to the protesters. In what would have basically been a repeat of the French Revolution that saw many of the royal troops join in with demonstrators, it was quite clear that Charles X only had one thing left to do: resign. Literally resigned to his fate, Charles X put in his resignation on August 2, 1830.

Shortly after that, he and his whole family left France to go into their self-imposed exile in England. His cousin, the duke of Orleans, Louis Philippe, succeeded him. Louis Philippe, the "citizen king," positioned himself not so much as the king of France but as the king of the French. He promised that he would be the standard bearer for the rights of the revolution that they so desperately craved.

He would respect the constitution and the freedom of the press and do his best to uphold the dignity of the French people, or so he claimed. His domestic strategy was to uphold the rights of the French, while his international strategy was to have close and strong alliances while avoiding unnecessary foreign entanglements. Bucking the tradition of centuries of animosity, the closest international ally that King Philippe sought out was Britain.

He most wished to emulate Britain in forming a constitutional monarchy, in which compromise and consideration of the public good was key. But no matter how much Philippe hoped he could find a winning balance of stability, it was not the case. Instead, his tenure as king was quite turbulent. He may have avoided outright revolution, but there were several episodes of protests, demonstrations, and even outright insurrections.

He also had to routinely shuffle the deck of his ministers. It is said that from August of 1834 to February of 1835, he went through five prime ministers. He also just barely dodged an assassination attempt on July 28, 1835. He was traveling from Tuileries to look at the National Guard, only to get shot at by a gunman who fired on him from a window of a nearby building. Even though the king escaped harm, several people were mowed down in the melee of bullets that tore into his entourage. This would not be the last attempt on Philippe's life, and he would face an assassin's attempt again in June of 1836.

In the meantime, Louis Napoleon, the nephew of Napoleon Bonaparte (who would later be dubbed "Napoleon III"), had been stirring up trouble. Using his name to provoke the Bonapartists, he attempted a coup in 1835 and tried again in 1840 before fleeing to Britain. When a series of uprisings and revolutions rocked much of Europe in 1848, Napoleon III found the perfect opportunity to return. No sooner than Philippe had abdicated from the throne on February 24, 1848, Napoleon III began to make waves again in France.

A provisional government was established, and an election for who would be the president of the "Second Republic" was launched. Napoleon III threw his hat in the ring and won in a landslide. He had excellent name recognition, of course, and thanks to the distance of several years between them and the events of the Napoleonic Wars, the hearts of many in the French public had grown rather fond of the old Bonaparte. The disasters that Napoleon Bonaparte had brought upon France during his reign were much forgotten, and those who wished to see the past through rose-colored glasses only remembered the prestige and greatness of Bonaparte.

It was these longings to be great once again that they projected onto the shoulders of his nephew Louis-Napoleon. And Louis, or as he preferred to be called, "Napoleon III," was ready to accept the expected mantle. Shortly after his election, he made sure to celebrate in the Elysée Palace, where his famous uncle had taken up residence in the past. Although perhaps many had empire-building on their minds when they considered the name of Napoleon, the first thing on Napoleon III's plate was not the building of an empire but the consolidation of what France already had.

His most pressing obligation was to fix the faltering French economy and the failing infrastructure. And in this feat, Napoleon III was surprisingly well suited for the task. It is said that under his tenure, France, which had been previously lagging behind its European counterparts, saw the ramping up of massive industrialization. Most importantly, Napoleon III saw new rail lines laid out throughout France. The fact that France finally acquired reliable, modern railroad transportation greatly impacted the French economy.

Now that goods could be easily transported from one part of the country to another, trade and commerce flourished. Wine in southern France, for example, could be easily shipped up to Paris, creating a veritable wine boom that did not exist before. There was no longer any need for local markets for wine when France's best wine could be shipped up from sunny, southern France any day of the week.

Railroad building, and other industrialization projects, were also positive developments as far as investment banks were concerned since they suddenly had a clearly defined field in which to invest their money. Investment banks' success led to an increase in general confidence in the banks, and more and more French citizens were putting both their faith and their money in banking institutions. Banknotes now had the complete confidence of the French people, and paper currency became the standard in France. All of these things were very important for the future of France and signaled many more positive things to come.

Perhaps due to his seemingly great economic and domestic success, when Napoleon III launched a coup in December of 1851 (to stay in power indefinitely), most of the French people seemed to take it all in stride. The only real pushback came from Napoleon III's former political opponent Victor Hugo, who led small demonstrations in Paris, but these were ultimately put down by Napoleon's troops and came to absolutely nothing.

The Second Republic had been rather quickly transformed into Napoleon III's personal empire. Such a thing should have been startling, but as long as the economy was booming, there would not be too many out in the streets to protest. On the contrary, Napoleon III did everything he could to present himself not as a tyrant but as the so-called "sovereign of the people." He was, in essence, a populist leader attempting to position himself as a man of the people with their best interests at heart.

Most seemed to be convinced that this was the truth. And even if they were not, Napoleon's rapidly expanding network of secret police likely would have made short work of them. As fine-tuned as the economy and domestic affairs seemed to be under Napoleon III, that is not to say that there were not any hiccups along the way. For it was in 1867 that the French lending institution, Credit Mobilier, failed.

But besides the banking collapse of Credit Mobilier, the worst setback that Napoleon III would face was his foreign policy. First, in 1862, during the height of the American Civil War, he backed a reckless expedition into Mexico, which installed Austrian Archduke Maximillian as the emperor of Mexico in 1864. This was supposedly done in retaliation for loans the Mexican government had failed to repay.

It is certainly not good for a country to fail in paying its debt, but most, then and now, would consider military occupation over defaulted loans a rather extreme choice to remedy the situation. And shortly after the Civil War ended, with the U.S. government no longer distracted by internal discord, France was told in no uncertain terms to keep its hands off of Mexico. This resulted in French troops leaving in 1867, even though Maximillian and his entourage attempted to stay, resulting in his arrest and death by firing squad.

Napoleon III likely wanted to put this debacle behind him quickly. But more failed foreign policy was to come. Since France had declared neutrality after the outbreak of hostilities between Prussia and Austria in 1866, they had been pulled ever closer to war with Prussia itself, a war that would erupt as the "Franco-Prussian War" in July of 1870. Napoleon III would prove to be disastrously unprepared for the masterful strategy of the Prussian leader Otto von Bismarck.

Napoleon would lose this war when on September 2, 1870, he and some eighty-four thousand soldiers were made to surrender after losing the Battle of Sedan. After this military defeat, Napoleon III finally faced personal defeat as leader of France. He was deposed, the empire was rendered null and void, and the French declared the coming of a Third Republic.

But even though France no longer referred to itself as an empire, it had enough sprawling territory to be considered imperial in scope. Despite its defeat in Europe, during the reign of Napoleon III, France had acquired considerable overseas territory. On the African continent, Algeria and Senegal had both become French colonies. The French took over modern-day Vietnam, Cambodia, and Laos in Southeast Asia, creating French Indo-China.

During this period, France also engaged in a pseudo-crusade by sending French troops to Lebanon, supposedly to protect Maronite Christians and Christian places of worship. Yes, France may no longer have called itself an Empire after the downfall of Napoleon III, but the imperial ambitions that France still projected onto much of the world at the end of the 19th century were indeed quite clear

Chapter 8: France's Long March toward the Guerre de Revanche

The Franco-Prussian War ended in a humiliating defeat. The National Assembly of France, which served as the acting authority of the nation at the time, signed its armistice with Prussia on January 28, 1871. This ended the Franco-Prussian War, but the bleak terms of the agreement would spark tremendous internal discord in France itself. The treaty had France lose European territories such as Alsace and Lorraine and had France fork out billions of francs in reparations.

However, the worst was yet to come when it was announced that the National Assembly would discontinue the salaries of the National Guardsmen stationed in Paris. The unrest of these harsh terms ignited massive protests in the streets of Paris and ultimately led to the Paris Commune, which came into spontaneous existence in March of 1871. The commune itself would be defended by those same National Guard troops who had been denied their paychecks.

The commune was a short-lived social experiment that would be forcefully put down that May. From March to May, Paris became a besieged encampment in which the Parisians (who had previously benefited from the railcars that regularly brought goods to the city) were forced to make do with whatever they had on hand. This led to dreadful scenes in which people in the city made meals out of cats, dogs, and sometimes even captured rats.

During these lean months, even the local zoo was not immune to the hunger of the demonstrators; at some point, even a couple of elephants were procured and butchered to supply meat for the besieged Parisians. On May 21, 1871, the loyal federal forces closed in, and the "bloody week" began, which saw the French regular army engage the National Guardsmen and their fellow revolutionaries, leading to the deaths of tens of thousands.

Although the commune was put down, its spontaneous eruption would leave a lasting impact on the likes of Karl Marx, who himself would later be considered the founder of *communism.* In his later writings on the subject, Marx considered the Paris Commune an example of a spontaneous eruption of what he called the "Dictatorship of the Proletariat." Marx viewed this event as an example of what might happen if the proletariat, or the average person on the street, took control of the government.

The threat of the commune allowed for the rise of French politician Adolph Thiers, who restored order and then took on the position of president and premier of the new French Republic. From this post, he managed to mitigate losses, and through the strategic use of so-called "loan drives," he was able to pay off 5 billion dollars' worth of reparations way ahead of schedule.

It was in 1872 that Thiers then set about remaking the French Republic in the most conservative image he could imagine. He reasoned that the French were tired of radical revolts, and the time for a restoration of the conservative status quo was in order. This was, in many ways, a return to the more conservative populism of Napoleon III, except without his imperial pretensions.

In many ways, French society has shifted back and forth between these two modes of thought since the days of the French Revolution. The French Revolutionaries were driven by the far left, only for a conservative backlash executed by Napoleon Bonaparte to come about. The revolutionaries of 1848 then led to much the same reaction by the factions of France championed by Napoleon III.

That said, the temporary uprising of the Commune of Paris can be viewed as the pendulum ever so briefly swinging back to the left before Adolph Thiers quickly turned it back to the right. By 1873, Thiers had been succeeded by Marshal MacMahon as president, who would remain so until he was forced to resign in 1879. Although ostensibly the "president" of the Republic, MacMahon was imbued with enough influence and power by France's monarchist faction, that many viewed him as a kind of uncrowned monarch.

Nevertheless, when a Republican majority was elected in the French Senate in 1879, he was indeed forced from power. Following the ouster of MacMahon, this particular spate of republican rule would last all the way until the year 1898. During this period, the infamous Dreyfus Affair erupted. The ordeal began in 1894 when an army officer named Alfred Dreyfus was accused of espionage, ultimately convicted, and exiled to Devil's Island.

However, even as those on the right congratulated themselves for a job well done, those on the left began to rail against the conviction as nothing short of political persecution at best and outright antisemitism at worst. Leading this charge was writer and activist Emile Zola. Zola's paper, *I accuse*, laid the case for what he believed to have been the framing of Dreyfus.

The arguments continued back and forth between the liberal left and the conservative right until Dreyfus was ultimately exonerated in 1906. The world was going through many changes, and alliances were shifting. By 1907, France had entered into the Triple Entente, in which France was firmly allied with Britain and Russia. This alliance was made to counteract what French officials viewed as the growing threat of Germany.

The German Empire had been declared after France had come out on the losing end of the Franco-Prussian War. Many are unaware of this fact, but the modern nation of Germany, as we know it today, did not exist until then. Before this, various German confederations and principalities existed in conglomerations such as the Holy Roman Empire and Prussia, but there was no "Germany."

It was in the aftermath of France's defeat that a unified German state was declared. Almost immediately, the new robust German nation on France's borders, which saw rapid increases in its military and economy, was a tremendous point of concern and anxiety for the French. As such, the French sought reassurance by entering into an alliance with Britain and Russia in case the Germans caused them any trouble. But as much as the French believed that this alliance brought them assurance, it also brought tremendous entanglement.

For not only were Britain and Russia obligated to come to France's aid, but France was also obligated to come to its partners' aid as well. This ensured that France could potentially be embroiled in conflicts with little or nothing to do with its own interests. And with the outbreak of World War I in 1914, this is more or less what happened. What interest did France have in declaring war on Germany simply because of German saber-rattling in the Balkans?

Yet, after one isolated incident in which a Serbian nationalist assassinated an Austrian duke, France was pulled into what would become World War One. The duke was killed, Austria made harsh demands, and when Serbia refused to meet them, Germany backed Austria's desire for reprisal. Russia, seeking to aid the Serbs, stood up to Germany. France was therefore obligated to stand up to Germany as well.

As the situation continued to spiral out of control, the lines of World War One would be drawn with the allies of Britain, France, and Russia, waging war against the so-called Central Powers of Germany, Austria, and the Ottoman Empire. As sudden as all of this was, some in France welcomed these developments. There was a movement known as the League of Patriots in particular, who had been clamoring for what they called "Guerre de Revanche" (a War of Revenge) to reclaim some of the prestige France had lost in 1870.

Yes, for some in France, their memories of past grievances were long, and even several decades later, the war erupting in 1914 seemed like an ample enough opportunity to reclaim lost ground. At the outset, the Allies and the Central Powers hoped for a quick and decisive war. But ultimately, the war would drag on in a bloody stalemate over the next few years.

The Germans had attempted to strike a lethal blow to the French by overrunning the low countries, driving through Belgium, and entering northern France. The goal was to push through all the way to Paris, but the French and their Allies successfully halted the German advance at the "Battle of the Marne." The Germans, it seems, underestimated the French fighting spirit. Although much of the French infrastructure had been damaged in the German drive south, the French troops had high morale and were determined to defend Paris. As such, they ferociously fought off the Germans.

Although the Germans would remain entrenched in northeastern France, thanks to the steadfast determination of the French army, they would not proceed any further. It was here on the so-called "Western Front" that much of the rest of this bloody war would be fought. The war would be fought hunkered down in the trenches with little to no change in territorial gains. Even so, the fighting was terrible and, at times, punctuated by poison gas. At the Battle of Ypres in April 1915, the Germans deployed poison gas against their enemies on the Western Front.

The next turning point of the war came with the bloody Battle of Verdun in 1916. The French troops were led by General Philippe Petain, who would later rise to infamy as the leader of Vichy France. However, during this period, he was the heroic leader of the French resistance to German aggression. Petain was a marvel of energetic action as he mobilized his troops in a seemingly non-stop effort to repel the Germans.

The French ultimately succeeded in this objective, but their victory came at a high cost of life. The war would drag on until the United States entered, eventually forcing the German front to collapse outright. The war finally ended with the singing of an armistice on November 11, 1918. This led to the Treaty of Versailles, which attempted to carve out the postwar order as the Allies saw fit.

According to this agreement, the French would see the repatriation of the Alsace-Loraine region that it had lost in the Franco-Prussian War. If this was the reward received for the Guerre de Revanche for many French, especially those who fought in the trenches, it must have seemed rather hollow.

For the Germans, the results would be even more bitter; Germany was militarily neutered, socked with heavy reparations, and subjected to the French occupation of the Rhineland. It was all of this bitterness that would serve as a prelude and sow the seeds for the next world war to come.

Chapter 9: La Resistance and Failing Colonialism

The seeds for World War Two had been planted shortly after the cessation of World War One. The war's end had left a bitter taste in the mouth of many who fought it, French and Germans included. The French at least could try and rationalize the tremendous loss of life with the notion that they had "won" the war. For the Germans, however, there was no such solace, only a sense of humiliated defeat.

It was these bitter feelings that Hitler and his Nazi party nourished as they gained prominence in the 1920s and then further reinforced when Hitler came to power in 1933. The French were well aware of the renewed German threat that they faced, but French leadership proved incredibly indecisive in how to deal with it. Even after Germany had rearmed and forcibly marched back into the Rhineland in March of 1936, neither the French nor their British allies did much of anything about it.

This hesitation to act only emboldened Hitler and his Nazis to become even more aggressive. There was a general desire among both the French and the British to avoid war, but the appeasement that resulted would ultimately bring about the very war that they were trying so hard to avoid. An emboldened Hitler began arbitrarily annexing nearby territories such as Austria and Czechoslovakia.

It was only when Hitler invaded Poland in 1939 that the British and the French were finally compelled to declare war on Germany. Germany then launched its blitzkrieg in May of 1940, which had German tanks rolling over the low countries of Belgium, Luxembourg, and the Netherlands, before penetrating into France.

The French were woefully unprepared for this onslaught and informed the British as much. The British, fearing French collapse, were ultimately forced to evacuate the forces they had in France. This led to the evacuation of hundreds of thousands of British troops from Dunkirk, France, as German troops closed in. France ultimately surrendered to Germany that June and ushered in what was referred to as the "Third Republic of France."

However, it was much more complicated than that since France was now essentially a divided nation. The Germans took over northern and western France outright, leaving only a rump state centered around Vichy. This new incarnation of France, subsequently dubbed "Vichy France," would be led by that ironclad French general of the First World War, Marshal Philippe Petain.

Although the Vichy government declared itself neutral, it was often enough coerced into being an active collaborator of the Nazis. The Nazis also successfully turned French sentiment against their former British allies. After the French fleet was destroyed by the British at the port of Mers El Kebir, for example, the Germans were able to use this as a propaganda club with which to hit the British over the head.

The British feared the Germans might get their hands on the French fleet, so they ordered the French to decommission their ships. When the French refused, the British launched an unprovoked attack against the French navy, blowing the French vessels out of the water. Obviously, this British attack was on a former ally and did not do much to improve relations with the French.

Nevertheless, French exiles in England had to somehow put such things behind them as they rallied toward the cause of "Free France." This movement of French exiles led by Charles de Gaulle would play a crucial role in the eventual liberation of France. So too, would the French resistance in France itself. The resistance of occupied France first conducted small-scale sabotage, such as destroying railroad tracks and phone cables. But after linking up with official contacts in Britain and among the Free French, a steady stream of both arms and intelligence allowed a truly underground army of resistance to form.

In the meantime, the Germans had severely overplayed their hand, despite their seemingly easy victories over Norway, the low countries,

France, and Poland. They were about to suffer from two strategic blows that would prove lethal. First, the German army invaded Russia. After rolling over Poland, the German high command somehow convinced itself that an invasion of Russia would be a walk in the park and launched the ill-fated Operation Barbarossa in June of 1941.

Seemingly forgetting all of the lessons of history, in particular, one learned by French dictator Napoleon himself, invading Russia's massive, frozen expanse is a formidable challenge logistically alone and likely doomed to failure. If this was not bad enough, Germany's ally Japan decided to attack Pearl Harbor, Hawaii, in December of 1941. This brought the United States into the war, not just against Japan but also against its partner, Germany.

The Germans, who previously only had England to worry about, now had both the United States and the Soviet Union fully committed to the war. The U.S. initially wanted to charge headlong into the German forces of mainland Europe by landing on the European continent in 1942. However, the British persuaded them not to do so and to strike out against the lower-hanging fruit of Axis power in North Africa.

This led to the Americans invading much of the North African territory of Vichy France, in Morocco, Algeria, and Tunisia. With the attack at Mers El Kebir still fresh in their minds, the naval forces of Vichy France were not exactly friendly to this incursion on their territory. Although the landings in Morocco faced little resistance, it is said that Algeria, in particular, had heavy pushback from the French stationed there.

Even so, the Allies prevailed and captured Vichy France Admiral Francois Darlan. Darlan proved a strategic boon because he agreed to work with the Allies toward a ceasefire of North African Vichy France forces as long as he was recognized as "High Commissioner for France and West Africa." Supporting Darlan, a clear collaborator, was not the most palatable of choices to have to make, but it was deemed to be important enough to do so.

Even so, many Free French leaders, including Charles De Gaulle, despised this decision. But Darlan, as fate would have it, would not have long in his tenure as High Commissioner since he was assassinated on December 24, 1942. The death of Darlan opened the door for De Gaulle to position himself as the leader of Free France, with a new base of operations established in Algeria.

The fact that a free French government had come into existence with the backing of the Allies on what was then technically French territory was a great propaganda victory for Free France. However, the Germans were not taking these developments lightly and had already moved to occupy France outright before the year was out.

Nevertheless, their stay would be brief.

The Allies eventually pulled off a successful landing in Normandy, France, on June 6, 1944, and the Free French led by Charles De Gaulle were right behind this liberation force. And this was not the end of the story as it pertains to the contributions made by the French troops during World War Two. The Free French and their allies from the underground would continue to battle the Germans all the way back to Germany, and as a result, upon Germany's defeat in 1945, the French would have their own occupied sector, along with the British, the Americans, and the Russians.

Not long after the war was over, one of these allies, the Russians, would be at odds with the rest, and a so-called Cold War between the communist East and the capitalist West would begin. The Soviet hold over East Germany would inspire the French, British, and Americans to combine their control sectors to unify into one Western German occupation zone.

France was having all kinds of problems with its faltering colonial holdings. Tensions were rising both in Algeria in North Africa, as well as in French Indochina in Southeast Asia. But of these locales, French holdings in Southeast Asia were the most pressing. French Indochina had actually been seized by the Japanese during the war. Japan was defeated along with its German and Italian allies, yet even after the Japanese were forced out, a local independence movement led by Ho Chi Minh was not about to let the French get back control.

Hi Chi Minh and his fellow cohorts in North Vietnam used communism as their vehicle to throw off the shackles of French colonialism. With the support of the Soviet Union and communist China, the Viet Minh of the north rallied at the Battle of Dien Bien Phu in 1954 and soundly defeated the French. This resulted in an agreement that had Vietnam split at the 17th parallel in recognition of communist North Vietnam and the newly established "Republic of Vietnam" in the south.

French Prime Minister Pierre Mendes-France realized that the days of French colonialism were numbered; as such, he laid out the groundwork for severing the ties that connected France to other overseas territories, such as Tunisia and Morocco, first granting them autonomy and then finally impendence in 1956. Even so, the French would hold off on releasing Algeria from the colonial ties that bind, with Mendes insisting that Algeria was "part of France."

Nevertheless, native Algerians felt otherwise, and after over one hundred years of French occupation, they, too, were ready for independence. The Algerians would struggle with the French in armed uprising after armed uprising until they finally shook off the French for good in 1962. In the meantime, the French had given up the ghost in Southeast Asia, handing over the baton to the United States, as a communist insurgency in South Vietnam backed by the North threatened to make all of Vietnam a haven for communism.

Unlike the French, the U.S. had no interest in colonialism, but because the insurgents were communist-based, Washington had deep fears of a communist domino effect spiraling out of control in the region. As such, U.S. officials did everything they could to support non-communist South Vietnam. They placed money and later personnel in the region to bolster its defenses against the communist north.

As early as 1954, the U.S. began sending over military advisors. It was not until 1965 that American forces committed themselves entirely to the conflict, a conflict they would ultimately lose in 1975. By this time, the French had washed their hands of Vietnam entirely. France would undergo a mini-Renaissance under that stalwart hero of the Second World War Charles De Gaulle, who came to power in France in 1958.

Mr. De Gaulle would work to forge a closer alliance with other European countries and bolster the French military, a program that included the establishment of a French nuclear arsenal, the latter of which was indeed very important to De Gaulle, who viewed it necessary to break up the virtual monopoly that the U.S. and the then Soviet Union had on nuclear weapons at this time. Even while asserting its independence as a newfound nuclear power, France also sought to strengthen its ties with its European neighbors.

This was especially true as it pertained to what was then known as "West Germany." Yes, even though the Germans had been the arch nemesis that had occupied and so horribly destabilized France, after the war, the rump state of West Germany would become the best friend of postwar France. Having half of their country sliced off and divided by a Berlin Wall, the Germans had their own problems, and the notion of solidarity with its European neighbors had become urgent.

As such, they eagerly signed a "friendship treaty" with France in 1963. But as much as De Gaulle courted closeness with Western European nations, he also courted controversy with the rest of the world. He alienated the United States with both statements and actions that seemed to indicate his desire to drift away from the lockstep that many other Western European states had with the U.S. during the Cold War.

De Gaulle's sudden denunciations of the Vietnam War were most infuriating from an American standpoint. Even though the Americans had essentially inherited the conflict from the French, De Gaulle made headlines in 1966 when he went on the record rejecting U.S. involvement in what he asserted was an "unjust war."

The following year, he managed to even infuriate Canadians when he visited Quebec in 1967 and made statements seeming to encourage French-speaking Quebec to assert its independence from the rest of Canada! And that was not the end of De Gaulle's international exclamation points. That same year, he also managed to enrage Israel and many of Israel's allies when he issued an arms embargo during the Six Day War.

Nevertheless, as much as De Gaulle wished to create a third option between siding with the United States on every issue or having to bow down to Soviet aggression, the genuine threats of the latter would soon make many of De Gaulle's positions seem ridiculous. The danger of Soviet aggression became all too real in 1968 when a demonstration in Czechoslovakia led to a vicious Soviet crackdown that included tanks rolling into Prague.

With the Soviets on the march, De Gaulle's drift away from U.S. foreign policy, which many viewed as being in the best interest of all Western nations, seemed tantamount to suicide at this point. Charles De Gaulle feeling the pressure of his own failed ambition, ultimately resigned from office in 1969. France had found itself adrift in new and uncharted territory and was looking for a friendly place to set anchor.

Chapter 10: France's Evolving Mission in a Globalized World

In its post-war years, France was finding itself as part of an increasingly interconnected and globalized world. Its colonial holdings might have been shed, but even without far-flung colonies, France was able to take full advantage of an increasingly internationalized marketplace that provided France access to an increasing area of goods and services.

But despite the more or less solid economic footing that France found itself on. The political footing was far from certain. Charles De Gaulle had ridden a wave of popularity in the 1960s only to resign in 1969. His resignation prompted a new election and a search for viable candidates. It was ultimately his own prime minister Georges Pompidou who became his successor. Although Pompidou was considered a "Gaullist," even though he was not Gaulle, many believed him to back similar policies and agendas.

But Pompidou proved to be much lower-key than his bombastic predecessor. He refrained from making incendiary remarks in public, and unlike De Gaulle, he expressed much more solidarity with France's traditional allies of Britain and the United States. Pompidou also followed a more traditional "laissez-faire" styled economy, allowing the market to work itself out of its own accord.

And by the 1970s, France was indeed experiencing an economic boom with robust international trade. As was demonstrated by the fact that the average French citizen now had their own cars, washing machines, refrigerators, and televisions. This is in stark contrast to the deprivation experienced in previous years. But perhaps most telling was the rush to equip French homes with phones.

Before Pompidou, only 14 percent of French homes had a working telephone. By the 1980s, however, it is said that that number had risen to 75 percent. It might seem a bit shocking to us today to think that France had been lagging behind the world in these commodities, but the gains made under Pompidou do give us a window into the lack that he encountered upon entering office.

Pompidou's exit was yet another sudden departure in French politics; he died in office on April 2, 1974. As many gains as his administration had made, he had left with a looming economic crisis due to the rising cost of oil. France was very much dependent on oil from the Mideast during this period, and an embargo put in place by oil-producing countries in 1973 led to severe inflation in 1974.

After Pompidou's demise, it was liberal leader Valery Giscard d'Estaing who would take on this economic crisis. Giscard did his best to stem the tide, but the problems seemed almost insurmountable. In the meantime, France would be rocked by yet another oil-fueled economic meltdown in 1979, in the wake of the Iranian Revolution. The west friendly Shah of Iran had been deposed and replaced with an Islamic regime.

Such things did not bode well for the upcoming election held in 1981. Here, the faltering Giscard faced off against the socialist stalwart Francois Mitterrand. Mitterrand was able to capitalize on the economic crisis and other turbulence that had erupted during the Giscard years and ran on a campaign of "*la force tranquille*," or "the tranquil force."

He presented himself as a calm, steady force that would be able to right the floundering French ship. Mitterrand's presentation was convincing enough, and he ultimately managed to squeak out a victory of 51.75 percent to Giscard's 48.24 percent. Now the 1980s belonged to the left wing of French politics. The question was, what would they do with it? The economy was still front and center, but Mitterrand also had some social objectives he wished to achieve.

His first major act while in office was to get rid of France's death penalty, which was officially eliminated from the French legal books in 1981. For a country known for the guillotine, the idea that no one in France, for political reasons or otherwise, would ever have to lose their head again was revolutionary in itself. As it pertains to the economy, the following year, in 1982, Mitterrand embarked upon an approach that probably did more for French finances than anything else during his tenure.

That year, he enabled local representatives at the municipal level to have much more robust control over the spending that went on in their districts. This helped create more oversight and was constructive in the fight against corruption. But it was perhaps Mitterrand's own socialist ambition that did in his administration. After he raised minimum wage, added in extra housing subsidies, medical benefits, and enhanced old age pensions, inflation began to go through the roof.

All of these social programs do not pay for themselves, of course. In a bid to offset their cost, Mitterrand had attempted to tax the wealthiest in France. Yes, in a classic imitation of Robin Hood, this socialist stalwart wished to rob the rich and give to the poor. But his efforts only added to France's already dire state of inflation.

It also did not help that Germany, the United Kingdom, and the United States were going in the opposite direction, enacting deflationary policies by raising interest rates. Soon France's inflationary spending was so out of control and its international interest rates so worthless that the franc itself became just about worthless, as the currency of France became repeatedly devalued.

Stats for economic growth in France from 1981 to 1984 show a growth rate of just 1.5 percent. Socialist or no socialist, Mitterrand was smart enough to know that his policies were not working, and by 1983, he was beginning to sing a different tune. At this point, his administration changed course and began to implement the same deflationary policies being executed by Western Europe and the United States.

On the international stage, the new realities of globalism and increased immigration to France from many of its former colonies were sparking anxieties in mainland France. These anxieties helped fuel the rise of right-wing nationalist, Jean-Marie Le Pen, and his party, the National Front. In light of the growing fear and discontent of the French electorate, the National Front began to gain traction.

At the same time, Mitterrand and his party did not seek to stoke fear and division but to kindle hope and solidarity among all French-speaking peoples across the globe. Starting in 1982, Mitterrand spearheaded international summits dedicated to the "Francophone nations," in which he spoke of his desire for universal understanding between these "carriers of [French] culture."

These efforts appealed to many in both French Canadian and African lands, where France was the dominant language. Mitterrand went into the 1988 elections with much uncertainty but managed to squeak out a win against his opponent Jacques Chirac. Mitterrand, in the meantime, was dealing with a faltering legacy. By the early 1990s, he was seeking anything upon which he could hang his political hat.

With this in mind, Mitterrand introduced proposals in 1992 for the French electorate to vote on the Maastricht Treaty, which was another significant step in European unification since it would help forge a universal European market. The measure passed but barely, with 59 percent voting for it and 49 percent voting against it.

The following year, however, the French economy took another hit when in 1993, French GDP declined, and unemployment skyrocketed. During the parliamentary elections of that same year, Jacque Chirac's party won seats in a landslide victory. This paved the way for Chirac's own election in 1995. Under the Chirac administration, economic conditions began to improve.

In 1998, for example, instead of contracting, the French economy is said to have hit a growth spurt, growing as much as 3.2 percent that year! France was doing well enough that the following year, it felt fully confident to lend its hand in the NATO conflict that had erupted over the former Yugoslavian country Kosovo.

After the eruption of the conflict in the spring of 1999, it is said that France supplied more aircraft fighter jets than any other European nation involved. Later that year, France also played a pivotal part in another step toward European unity by supporting the creation of the "Eurozone" in 1999. France faced an economic downturn in the early 2000s; however, it went bust after the dot-com boom.

The situation was so bad that taxi drivers went on strike in the cities, and farmers used their tractors to block off access to oil refineries. Going into the 2002 election, the situation looked grim, yet Jacques Chirac stunned the world by coming out on top with a landslide win of 82 percent of the vote. The explanation for this feat was simply that there were no other candidates that were at all palatable to the French electorate.

Chirac's main competitor was socialist politician Lionel Jospin and far-right hopeful Jean Marie Le Pen. No one was thrilled with Jospin, and no one was willing to vote a far-right candidate like Le Pen into office. This does much to explain Chirac's landslide win. Even so, the fact that a character like Le Pen picked up as much of the vote as he did prompted the satirical French TV show "Les Guignols d l'Info" to do a skit with a La Pen puppet quietly standing around in the background.

The Le Pen puppet was asked what it was up to, only for it to answer, "Nothing–just waiting." As if all the far right had to do was wait for the French to lose faith in France's more traditional political parties, and the door to the presidency would be opened for them.

Shortly after the election, when the U.S. launched its ill-fated 2003 invasion of Iraq, Chirac inflamed tensions with the U.S. by refusing to participate. Although U.S. President George W. Bush had traveled the world making the case that Iraq had weapons of mass destruction and was connected to terrorist groups, Chirac saw neither the connection nor the necessity of the invasion.

As history would later attest, Chirac seems to have made a wise choice. Iraq was found not to have the weapons of mass destruction that the Bush administration had suggested. And any active connection to terror groups was never adequately proven. Even so, the fact that France snubbed the United States' war efforts would put a dent in U.S./French relations.

In 2007, Chirac was succeeded by his former Prime Minister Nicolas Sarkozy. Although France had sat out the 2003 invasion of Iraq, it did recognize the need to beef up its military. And in 2008, one of the first initiatives Sarkozy embarked upon was modernizing the French army. This meant heavy investment in modern drones, satellites, the latest jet fighters, and even the construction of new nuclear submarines.

Interestingly, even though the French military stayed its hand during the Iraq war, in 2011, during the so-called "Arab Spring" that rocked North Africa, when rebels toppled Kaddafi in Libya, Sarkozy sent in some of those aforementioned fighter jets to lend his support. The reasons for doing this could be argued to be just as questionable as the reasoning behind the invasion of Iraq, but in this instance, Sarkozy decided not to be shy with the use of the French armed forces.

Sarkozy would not win reelection; however, he ultimately lost the presidency to Francois Hollande in 2012. Hollande would, in turn, be succeeded by French President Emanuel Macron in 2017. Macron was then reelected in a nail-biter of an election in 2022. He was running against the older La-Pen's daughter Marine Le Pen. Macron was the first incumbent French president to win reelection since the days of Jacques Chirac back in 2002.

Conclusion: Rising to the Challenge

France is one of the planet's oldest, continuous hubs of human habitation. We must say "human habitation" because although the name "France" has not always been applied to this region, human dwellers have been on the land for many millions of years. As those who inhabited this land first began to show up in the annals of recorded history, they were known as Gauls, and France itself became the land of Gaul as far as the Romans were concerned.

After the fall of the Roman Empire from which ancient France had been incorporated, a tribe known as the "Franks" came to prominence, and it was from them that the name "France" was ultimately derived. Under the Franks, we first saw the Merovingian, the Carolingian, and finally, the Capet dynasties that would bring a long line of French kings to the throne.

This procession of royal administrations would be interrupted by the French Revolution, which would rock not just France but also society in general to its very core. The French Revolution would bring forth tremendous bloodshed, as kings, queens, and the average citizen alike were all trampled under the wheels of revolutionary fervor.

But even so, the French Revolution, despite the violence that it brought about, also enshrined some of the most enduring aspects of modern law, such as a free press and individual rights that today many in the Western world take for granted. Even so, the drafters of these laws would not always enjoy them. The Revolution would ultimately devolve into a dictatorship under Napoleon Bonaparte, and Bonaparte would lead much of the world into battle against him.

After the Napoleonic wars finally came to a close, with Napoleon's final abdication in 1815, France would temporarily go back to the Bourbon monarchy. However, this was just a brief interlude before Napoleon III would rise to the throne in the aftermath of the wave of revolutions in 1848. Napoleon III sought to rebuild his uncle's empire, and in many ways, he was successful. It was under Napoleon III that France would regain much of its lost prestige through military successes and the acquisition of territory all over the globe.

Napoleon III would be toppled in 1870 by rising German power in the form of Prussia. The toppling of the French would have significant ramifications in the form of the unification of Italy and Germany. France's days of Empire in Europe seemed to be over, but its colonial empire remained. This it would not lose until World War Two forced much of France's overseas holdings out of its hands.

In the aftermath of World War Two, France tried its best to recoup and regain some of its lost overseas territory, especially Vietnam and Algeria, but ultimately had to wash its hands of them. With the loss of its past imperial possessions, France began to turn inward and ultimately began to look toward the European neighborhood for the future.

It was around this time, of course, that the first steps toward the European Union began. France was always at the forefront of this charge, first with the establishment of the European Commission and then the creation of the Eurozone; all of these things helped to forge what we now call the EU.

France continues to lead the way no matter what factors are in play or the situation. France has always played a unique role in the region, and its mission continues to evolve. That said, France faced significant turbulence in the late 2010s, with an upsurge of terror attacks aimed at destabilizing French society.

First, there was the Charlie Hebdo attack in January 2015, only to suffer through the November terror attacks that were staged in Paris, killing over one hundred people. There was also a truck bomb attack in

Nice, France, in 2016, just prior to Emanuel Macron's rise to power in 2017. These are some pretty fierce headwinds for anyone to deal with. Even so, judging from France's long history, the land of the Franks will undoubtedly rise to the challenge.

Part 2: The French Revolution

An Enthralling Guide to a Major Event in World History

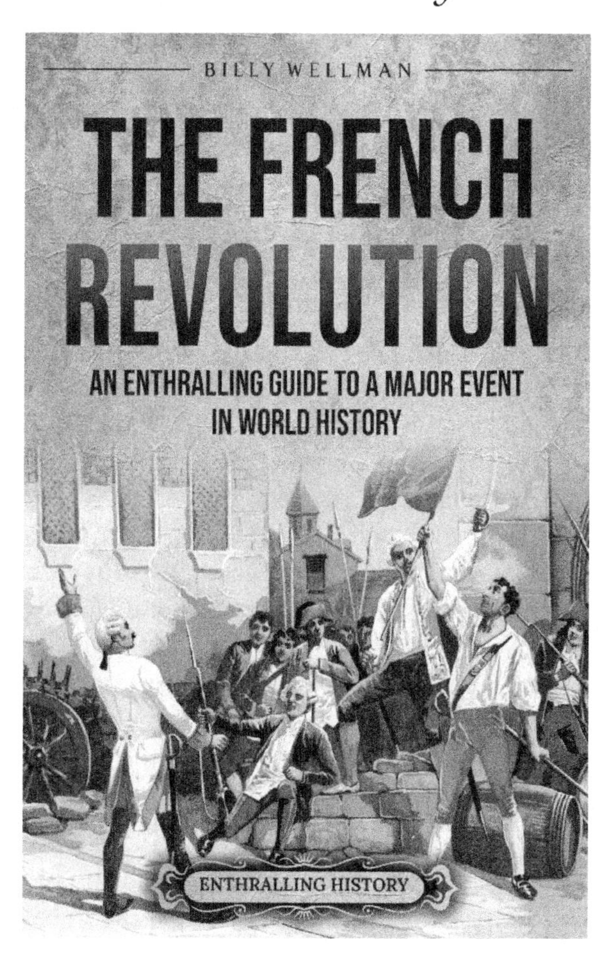

Introduction: The French Revolution—What Happened?

The French Revolution stands out as one of the most pivotal moments in history, not just because of what happened in France but also because of how it affected the rest of the world. The undercurrents of what was taking place in France would shake up much of the known world.

As the ideals of the French Revolution spilled outside of French borders, the nations of Europe and the Americas began to absorb them. The lines of European nations were redrawn, while colonial powers, such as Spain and Portugal, lost their hold over their American possessions. Latin America was perhaps the most affected, as country after country in Latin America declared its independence in the aftermath of the French Revolution.

However, even more importantly, the French Revolution disrupted common thought. Before the French Revolution had begun, French intellectuals frequently poked and prodded at the social, religious, and political conventions of the day.

This is perhaps no better demonstrated than in the French Revolution's effect on what was then a centuries-old practice—the Inquisition. The first Inquisition began in the late 12th century, although things really picked up with the Spanish Inquisition, which began in the 15th century. Grand inquisitors were sent from town to town, making inquests into those who were accused of being non-Christians. They had the power and authority to torture and kill if necessary in their quest for "the truth."

It is perhaps a little-known fact, but just prior to the French Revolution, French philosophers like Voltaire played a key role in spreading the word about the abuses and trespasses of the Inquisition. Voltaire would not live to see the French Revolution, but many of his thoughts were put into action during that time and might have helped lead to the end of the Inquisition, which he had so regularly harangued.

Ironically (but perhaps not so coincidentally), the French despot Napoleon Bonaparte brought much of the brutality of the Spanish Inquisition to an end. When his armies conquered Spain, he issued orders to shut it down. The French Revolution's impacts are indeed deep and incredible to contemplate. In this book, we explore the major aspects of the French Revolution and its subsequent impact on the larger world.

Chapter 1: Before the Revolution

"Every time I appoint someone to a vacant position, I make a hundred unhappy and one ungrateful."

-King Louis XIV

To understand the French Revolution, we need to take into account the events that occurred prior to its outbreak. French society had become increasingly unstable in the decades leading up to the revolution. The French Crown had fought a series of losing wars against Britain, the last of which–the Seven Years' War–saw France lose considerable territory in North America, such as Quebec.

This was a humiliation for French pride and proved to be a drain on the French economy as well. The French had to pay the costs accrued from a failed war and suffer the loss of revenue from their former North American colonies. In the meantime, French society was becoming increasingly unequal. There had always been distinct social classes in France, but as the economy was being run into the ground, corruption took hold.

For those who had the extra cash on hand, important posts could be bought. This created a situation in which the wealthy could buy their way into positions of power and lord it over the rest. The worst of this pay-for-play phenomenon occurred in the guilds.

During the Middle Ages and into the early modern period, many European countries had an established set of guilds or trades that certain people did. There were carpenter guilds for carpenters, shipbuilding guilds for shipbuilders, tailor guilds for tailors, and so on and so forth.

These guilds previously only had the best of the best within their ranks. But as corruption set in, it became possible to gain access to a guild by simply buying one's way into it.

One can only imagine the chaos this created when the son of a rich noble could suddenly become a carpenter just because he wanted to be a carpenter, not because he had the skills necessary for that vocation. For the right sum of money, anyone could buy their way into a guild. This caused French trade to become inefficient, stifled free enterprise and creativity, and led to widespread discontent.

Just imagine someone today approaching a hospital board and stating, "Hey, my son really wants to be a doctor." The son doesn't have the right qualifications, but after his rich parents hand over a million dollars, they pull enough strings to get him licensed as a surgeon. Due to this terrible instance of corruption, we now have someone doing open heart surgery who doesn't even know how to use a scalpel!

This was precisely the kind of corruption that had become common practice in the guild systems of pre-revolutionary France. However, even worse was the so-called "sale and purchase of offices." The French had developed a long-standing tradition of government posts and offices being sold to the highest bidder. According to historian Simon Schama, "the sale and purchase of office was more deeply and broadly rooted in France than in any other major power in Europe."

Schama asserts that the practice has its roots in actions undertaken by King Henry IV of France back in 1604 when the French monarchy embarked upon a scheme to sell prestigious government posts to raise much-needed funds for the French treasury. This sort of corruption—the notion that one could buy their way into either positions of power or an esteemed guild—would eventually rot the core of any good society, and that is precisely the sort of thing we see at work in pre-revolutionary France.

As the guilds became worthless, the only way the government could stave off complete economic collapse was by writing off debt through annuities. There were all kinds of government-backed schemes, such as so-called "perpetual annuities," "life annuities," and, at one point, even revertible annuities. It did not matter what gimmick the French king's finance ministers tried, as they were playing with fire. In reality, they were just delaying what would become an inevitable financial collapse.

The French monarchy, due to its extravagance and poor management, had long squandered the resources of what had once been a thriving French presence on the world stage. King Louis XIV, also known as the Sun King, reigned for seventy-two years, from 1643 to 1715. While France emerged as a leading power during his rule, he also set a precedent for how a king should live. Granted, he had the funds to do this, as he made sound reforms early in his reign. However, France became engaged in several major wars, and Louis sought to decrease the nobles' power. As the years passed, Louis XIV needed more money, and he wanted to tax the aristocrats to get it. It was not a popular move, and the taxes ended up being ineffective, with the nobles finding ways to get out of paying them.

King Louis XV had to strengthen the economy in some way, but his taxes on the nobility were not effective either. France fought in more wars. But where Louis XIV won his wars, Louis XV lost many of his. France was in a state of chaos before Louis XVI even took the throne. If France was going to succeed, it needed a strong ruler at the helm.

King Louis XVI was not that strong ruler. This is not to say that Louis XVI was the worst ruler who ever lived. If he had ruled at a different point in history, he likely would have had a semi-successful reign. He could make smart decisions, but he didn't know how to make the people follow his reforms. He also followed in the footsteps of his family, spending money to keep up appearances and engaging in more frivolous activities like hunting.

A great example of this would be his coronation in 1775 when he refused to tone down the extravagance of the ceremony, even after the Controller General of France, Anne Robert Jacques Turgot, advised that he would be wise to do so. Just prior to Louis XVI being crowned, there had been terrible grain riots and unrest in the streets over rising prices. In light of these difficulties, Turgot felt that not only should extravagance be minimized but that it would also serve the king best to hold the coronation in Paris, where the average discontent Parisian could see him, rather than hold the ceremony in the faraway and disconnected opulence of Reims Cathedral.

According to historian Simon Schama, the switch to a more low-key gathering in Paris likely would have saved seven million livres. The cost of having to transport everything, including skilled Parisian artisans, was a major drain on finances.

The costly royal apartments set up temporarily in Reims also sparked tremendous criticism, especially when it was learned that the queen had gone out of her way to install what historian Schama refers to as "English water closets." In other words, this temporary yet costly abode in Reims came decked out with plumbing, including an early version of a functioning toilet. At this time, most French people were stuck using chamber pots.

Such things did not bode well for the new king, who seemed out of tune with the French people from the outset. Besides being costly, some aspects of the ceremony verged on the absurd, such as when sacred oil, supposedly dating back to the first French king (Clovis, King of the Franks), was liberally applied to Louis XVI.

The French king, Louis XVI, would later go on to support the American rebellion against the British Crown, but it was not because he agreed with the American revolutionaries' principles. Far from it. Instead, he simply supported the colonists because it was a way for him to get back at his enemies, the English, who had robbed him of his colonies in the Seven Years' War. For the French ideologues back home, the irony could not have been thicker. The idea that the Americans could achieve the freedom they sought while they were expected to suffer in silence under their own tyrannical king seemed beyond absurd.

As such, the movement to depose King Louis XVI grew. The discord was the most palpable in the French capital of Paris. Exacerbating tensions was a large wave of migrants from the countryside flocking to the capital in search of better work opportunities.

Initially, this seemed to present a potential economic boon, as new factories were developed, and industrialization was encouraged by this large labor pool. The jobs were filled so rapidly by this influx of new arrivals that many of the job seekers had to be turned away, leaving empty-handed. And when work could not be found, the increased population of Paris proved to be more of a burden than a benefit. The French government seemed to shift between trying to aid the newcomers and trying to prohibit them. Many new laws were issued that restricted movement in a last-ditch effort to curtail the steady migration to Paris. However, it was too little, too late, and the French king soon had a large mass of discontented people right on his doorstep demanding that he do something to alleviate their many woes.

And the woes of the poor peasants in France were indeed many. The conditions of the lower classes were shockingly threadbare compared to other European countries of the time. French peasants typically lived in rundown houses that lacked even a proper floor. Rather than wooden floorboards, most of them were just floorless shacks—walls and a roof—roughly assembled on the dirt. The peasants' diet was not much better. They hardly ever had meat, and their meals primarily consisted of bread and perhaps a few vegetables.

It is worth noting that bread played a major part in the French Revolution in many ways. At first glance, the notion that bread was a major factor in a revolution may sound a little absurd, but it is true. The French, especially the French peasants, depended on a steady supply of bread to survive.

And as the prices of bread rose and fell, so did the stability of the French government. There were countless bread riots leading up to the revolution. In January 1789, on the very eve of the French Revolution, bread prices doubled, and the calls for revolutionary reform reached a fever pitch.

When King Louis XVI and his queen, Marie Antoinette, were deposed, the people were heard chanting that they would no longer want for bread because they had just captured the bakers. Crowds were heard rejoicing, "We are bringing back the baker and the baker's wife!"

Such notions were terribly misguided and overly simplistic. If anyone really thought having a captive French king on their hands would give them a lifetime supply of bread, they would soon learn how terribly mistaken they were. The troubles of the French peasants persisted after the king and queen were captured and even after their execution.

Marie Antoinette is often quoted as having said "Let them eat cake" when her ministers pestered her and her husband about the price of bread. However, it is widely believed that she never uttered those words. Still, she was out of touch with what the majority of the French populace was facing, but so were all the other nobles. And in the lead-up to the French Revolution, it seemed that just about everyone had their complaints and criticisms, but very few had any real solutions.

On the eve of the French Revolution, the French government was straining under immense debt. Much of this debt was due to the costs of previous wars. Both the Seven Years' War and the French commitment to supporting the Americans during the American Revolutionary War had racked up considerable debt. France's previously mismanaged policies did not help things either. As it pertained to fiscal responsibility, a big part of the problem lay at the feet of the absolute monarchy. In England, Parliament served as a guardrail when it came to monetary policies. But in France, everything was carried out at the monarch's whim. There were no restrictions in place to hold him back; really, the only thing that could stop him would be a coup or a revolution.

As historian Simon Schama put it, "In France, there was no comparable institution that could act as a dependable watchdog and so reassure future depositors and creditors of government." England had Parliament standing guard, but who would keep the French king in check? It was this fact that made investors more than a little nervous about investing in France.

At any rate, the French government sought to recoup some of its debt by resorting to high taxation. This created more discontent at just about every level of French society. At one point, even the French clergy protested. In 1775, they determined their annual stipends were not sufficient enough to combat inflation and the rise in taxes.

Before the French Revolution, the French government had become corrupt and rotten to its core. It was clear that something had to be done. The sentiments that change was necessary would drive the revolution forward. And French philosophers had been calling for this change for some time.

French philosopher and firebrand Voltaire was at the forefront of this push. Voltaire was a highly influential figure, even though he did not live to see it all play out. Even though it took about another ten years after his death for the revolution to break out, he could sense what was about to happen. Voltaire, thinking that an age of democracy, freedom, and prosperity was about to be ushered in, was envious of those who would live to see it.

In 1764, Voltaire famously declared, "Everywhere the seeds are being sown of an inevitable revolution which I shall not have the joy of witnessing. Happy are the young, for they will see great things!"

Voltaire perished at the age of eighty-three in the year 1778, about ten years prior to the outbreak of the French Revolution. If Voltaire had lived to see the aftermath of the French Revolution, he likely would have regretted his remarks.

As an indication of how much French thought would transform by the eve of the revolution, Voltaire, who was very much considered a liberal during his lifetime, would have been considered a conservative by the time the French Revolution broke out.

For example, Voltaire railed against the abuses of the Catholic Church, specifically the inquisitions that were taking place in Spain, Portugal, and Rome. However, Voltaire was not against religion itself. On the contrary, he himself professed belief in God and insisted that religion was good as long as it was natural and not forced on people. This would be very different from what took place during the French Revolution.

In the wake of the French Revolution, the church was attacked and even threatened with annihilation, as Maximilien Robespierre and his cronies tried to "invent" a new religion they could force upon the whole French state. This madness was ultimately stopped. Napoleon Bonaparte, of all people, restored the Catholic Church's hegemony over France.

Voltaire likely would have looked on in horror as these things played out. And who knows? Perhaps Voltaire would have been forced to pay a visit to the guillotine before it was all over. Such a thing would not be surprising, considering all of the people who were suddenly deemed expendable due to the irrational whims of fervent revolutionaries.

Voltaire is just one of the heavyweight French thinkers who come to mind when considering some of the inspirations behind the French Revolution. However, Voltaire did not advocate for the outright overthrow of the French monarchy. Instead, he advised a more cautious approach that would transform the absolutist rule into a constitutional monarchy.

Voltaire lived in Britain as a young man and absorbed much as it pertains to the British way of life. He often spoke of his admiration for the British embrace of merit (no matter how limited it might have been) while heaping scorn on French nobles who used money and aristocratic birth to foist their will on others. Early in his career, in the year 1733, Voltaire made use of his many observations and compiled them into a piece entitled *Letters on the English*, in which he praised certain aspects of British society while taking subtle swipes at France.

In one passage, for example, he speaks rather glowingly of British methods of taxation, stating, "No one is exempted in this Country [England] from paying certain taxes because he is a nobleman or a priest."

Voltaire's readers back home in France would have readily recognized this statement as an indirect criticism of the French way of life. In France, it was common knowledge that certain members of the nobility and clergy were often exempt from paying taxes. Even though the swipes were subtle, this work and others by Voltaire and his peers enraged the French monarchy. They saw Enlightenment thinkers like Voltaire as nothing but a direct threat to their own authority.

Nevertheless, an undercurrent of intellectual thought bubbled under the surface for some time in France, an undercurrent that would do its utmost to influence and mobilize the unhappy French masses. And the masses were indeed many. France, despite all of its problems, boasted one of the biggest populations in Europe.

Just prior to the revolution, France is said to have had a population of some twenty-eight million people. During this period, Britain barely had a population of ten million. Russia had a population of around thirty million, but one has to keep in mind that Russia's landmass is much larger than that of France. France's current population is about twice as much as it was back then, but modern-day France is also much more capable of coping with a larger population than it was in the late 18th century. Plus, the modern-day French population is more evenly distributed throughout the country.

Pre-revolutionary France found itself low on resources and revenue with a huge, ever-growing population crowding into its cities. The French intelligentsia set to work to address these problems. But little did any of those well-meaning revolutionary ideologues know about the Pandora's box they were about to open.

And in this backdrop, the Estates General would convene. The Estates General was France's legislative body made up to represent the various "estates" of France. The French public of that time was broken up into three main categories. The First Estate was made up of the clergy, the Second Estate the nobility, and the Third Estate comprised the vast bulk of France. The Third Estate was everyone who did not fit into the other two categories; farmers, merchants, shop owners, and blacksmiths, just to name a few, would have all been part of the Third Estate.

The Estates General convened to discuss some of the most pressing problems facing France on May 5th, 1789. The convening of the Estates General was meant to soothe rattled nerves, but all it seemed to do was stir things up. King Louis XVI initiated the discussion, speaking to all of those assembled and attempting to address the many problems the nation faced.

Another important figure, the finance minister, Jacques Necker, spoke before the crowd about the dire circumstances facing the French economy. Necker's go-to solution of enforcing higher taxes predictably fell flat with those who had assembled. Taxes were already high, and it was largely the Third Estate who shouldered the burden.

The Third Estate was upset for another reason. In past sessions of the Estates General, each estate got one vote. The First Estate and the Second Estate tended to side together, leaving the Third Estate, even though it was the most numerous, out in the cold. They wanted to fix things so that every delegate present got a vote. Well, the king had more important things on his mind (taxes), and the discussion of representation was never really talked about.

Frustrated with the situation, members of the Third Estate created a new legislative body, which would become known as the National Assembly. This was all done without the consent of the king. The Third Estate began to refer to themselves as the Communes in reference to their "common" status. They considered their numbers to be of greater significance than any perceived clout or status that the clergy and nobility held.

The gathered representatives of the Third Estate considered themselves the true representatives of the nation, thus forging a true National Assembly to represent French interests. The king sought to shut down what he viewed as an unlawful assembly. He even shut down the meeting hall where the group had convened in the hopes that they would disperse.

However, the Communes simply moved their deliberations to a local tennis court, where they took part in the so-called "Tennis Court Oath," in which they promised not to depart until they had successfully forged a new constitution for their nation. Although no shots had yet been fired, this was indeed the start of what would become an all-out revolution.

Chapter 2: The Storming of The Bastille

"Smuggle out the truth, pass it through all the obstacles that its enemies fabricate; multiply, spread by all means possible her message so that she may triumph; through zeal and civic action counterbalance the influence of money and the machinations lavished on the propagation of deception. That, in my opinion, is the most useful activity and the most sacred duty of pure patriotism."

-Maximilien Robespierre

The French might still recognize Bastille Day as one of their great holidays and hallmarks of their long march toward liberty, but the Storming of the Bastille was by no means a pretty picture. It happened as a result of the restless peasants wanting to arm themselves against the French government.

Before the Bastille, a large fortress and prison, was stormed, the French king had mobilized troops against ongoing bread riots and other demonstrations. He then began cleaning house in his own government. His actions culminated in the termination of Jacques Necker, the finance minister, on July 11th, 1789.

In many ways, Necker had been instrumental in his own demise. He was tasked with fixing the huge debt accrued by France in its effort to aid the American Revolution. Some tried to put the blame on Necker himself, and there was grumbling that he was "cooking the books."

In an effort to come clean on how much was owed, Necker took the step of making the national budget public, which was unusual for an absolute monarchy. Typically, state finances were kept quiet. The memorandum Necker issued was known as the *Compte rendu*. This report shed new light on the French government's state of affairs, alerting the public to all of the dire details of the French economy.

Necker then sought to make taxation more equal by dividing up the taille and capitation taxes. The capitation tax was a poll tax on property, while the taille tax was a more direct form of taxation aimed at the peasant classes in France. While it wasn't unheard of for the more affluent to pay the taille tax, the clergy and nobility typically got out of it by claiming to have a tax-exempt status. This created an increasing hatred of the taille tax, which came to be viewed essentially as a "poor tax" forced upon the lower classes of France.

Although Necker's proposal of reforming the taille tax was popular with many of the poorer French, it alienated the elites, who normally would have been Necker's most important and powerful patrons.

As soon as the people learned that Necker had been terminated, a ripple of panic went through investors. In their minds, the dismissal of the finance minister seemed to indicate the whole country was about to go bankrupt. The elites in France began to raise the alarm.

So, now the poor and the rich were discontented. In the immediate aftermath of Necker's dismissal, which occurred on July 11th, 1789, Paris became ground zero for a revolution.

There was a strange dichotomy in the works, with the National Assembly of France—a special representative body established in the first stages of the French Revolution—seeking to urge calm, even while increasingly upset crowds of people began to gather in the capital. The National Assembly had signed the Tennis Court Oath in direct defiance of the French king, who had ordered them to disband. With this act of defiance, the National Assembly showed that the French monarchy was losing control of this rapidly unfolding situation.

There is nothing worse for a country than to have a mob of unemployed, hungry, and agitated folks roaming throughout the streets, yet that was exactly what Paris, France, looked like at this point in time. And once the people learned of the finance minister's removal, they went into action. Seeming to think that no finance minister meant no control of finances, mobs stormed into toll houses and other tax-collecting institutions, seeking to take back the money they felt had been taken from them.

The king's troops could have fired upon the crowds since they were clearly breaking the law. But as is the case with any breakdown of society, a turning point was reached. Instead of firing on the agitated protesters, the troops shrugged their shoulders, turned their backs, and looked the other way.

With the French soldiers having lost the will to repress their angry countrymen, they opened the door to all kinds of mayhem and lawlessness. Although the French soldiers were unwilling to discharge their weapons to protect the social order, the rabble in the streets was more than willing to seize arms to disrupt it.

On July 13th, 1789, a large crowd assembled in the main town hall in Paris and openly asked for weapons. They insisted they needed these weapons to "protect the city" since the French soldiers had proven themselves unwilling to do so. They were initially met with refusal, but soon enough, administrators began to cave in. It was then agreed that the electors of Paris, who served as representatives, would be allowed to establish a people's militia.

The electors were initially convened to elect the deputies to represent Paris's Third Estate, but in the drama that had unfolded, they became a kind of revolutionary committee that made demands on behalf of the demonstrators. At the behest of the electors, an allotment of rifles and ammunition was distributed to the people, but it was soon deemed not to be worthy of the effort.

The protestors wanted more, and they knew where to get it: the Bastille. The Bastille was a fortress that held prisoners, weapons, and ammunition. The French knew that if they could gain access to the Bastille's armory, they would be well armed. The electors leading the protests ultimately decided to move against the Bastille on the following day, July 14th.

Even though the demonstrators were numerous in number, the storming of the Bastille would not be an easy task. The Bastille stood tall between thick walls and was surrounded by a moat. Initially, the leaders of the mob tried a somewhat diplomatic approach. They stood at the gates of the Bastille and attempted to negotiate with the governor of the Bastille, Bernard-René Jourdan de Launay. They asked him for arms. In the midst of these talks, someone—it is not entirely clear who—opened fire. This led to the whole armed guard at the Bastille opening up on the protesters. Hundreds were killed, but the mob kept coming until the Bastille was overwhelmed.

With so many of their comrades dead, the rage of the protestors was uncontrollable. Right before the protestors were about to break down the doors, Governor de Launay agreed to surrender on the promise that he and those with him would be spared. However, when the Bastille was surrendered, all promises were forgotten.

De Launay was marched outside and horrifically abused. People in the crowd beat him and spit on him. Revolutionary leaders were still trying to figure out what to do with him when Launay, weary of the misery he was being put through, shouted that they should kill him. According to historian Simon Schama, he shouted, “Let me die!”

Launay apparently sought to provoke his death by kicking one of the men closest to him—a fellow whose name comes down to us as Desnot—in the groin. After this outburst, several men leaped on him, tearing him to pieces with swords, daggers, and whatever else they had on hand.

His body was hacked into pieces, and his decapitated head was placed on top of a pike and victoriously thrust into the air by the bloodthirsty crowd. This was an altogether terrible episode, and, in many ways, it was a foreshadowing of the rest of the horror to come.

Along with the desire to acquire weapons, the mob had been partially inspired to storm the Bastille on rumors that it was filled to the brim with prisoners who had dared to speak ill of the regime. In reality, the Bastille is said to have only housed seven prisoners at the time, and none of them were being held for their political views. Word of what happened spread relatively fast, and soon, there were similar demonstrations popping up all over France.

One of the more interesting elements in this early stage of the revolution was the prominent role women played. While it is true that women were generally shut out of the inner circles of revolutionary thought, which forged new civil laws and a constitution, female protesters played a very important role and were quite visible in the streets of France. In the fall of 1789, this was evident when some seven thousand women marched on Versailles, the seat of the French government, where the king resided.

On October 5th, 1789, an angry mob primarily composed of women reacted to high bread prices by marching through the streets of Paris, shouting, "When will we have bread?" This was the title of a protest pamphlet that had been passed out by firebrand intellectuals.

As writer and historian Simon Schama put it in his groundbreaking text *Citizens: A Chronicle of the French Revolution*, "Early on the fifth, the tocsin was rung from the Church of Sainte-Marguerite and, led by a woman beating a drum, a march formed, the crowd shouting the title of the latest pamphlet, *When Will We Have Bread?* As they marched, they recruited women from other districts, many of them carrying cudgels, sticks and knives. By the time they had converged on the Hôtel de Ville the crowd was some six or seven thousand strong."

One can only imagine this strange scene of thousands of women marching with knives, clubs, and, in some instances, sticks, shouting and screaming that they needed bread while liberally abusing their least favorite French monarch, Queen Marie Antoinette.

But why was Marie Antoinette so thoroughly reviled by the French people? This requires some explanation. Initially, the disdain of Marie Antoinette was quite petty. From the start of her public life as queen, many resented the fact that she was not French. As narrow-minded as it sounds, the French public simply did not warm up to the fact that Louis XVI had married a woman who hailed from Austria.

This general disdain was greatly amplified by the French press through a steady series of digs and jabs at her character. All of this negative gossip culminated when the queen was falsely accused of taking an immensely expensive necklace and not paying for it, thereby defrauding the Crown jewelers. This accusation caught on like wildfire in the gossip mills of France, and everyone who already disliked the queen used this piece of gossip to validate their own prejudice.

The accusations were false, and it was later found that the queen's signature had been forged, making it seem as if she had agreed to purchase the necklace when she had not. Nevertheless, Marie Antoinette's reputation had already been ruined, and she would be the butt of jokes and a target of the people's hatred all the way up until she lost her head by way of the guillotine.

Misguided or not, by the time the massive throng of demonstrators arrived at the Hôtel de Ville, their demands had been ratcheted up considerably. Along with complaining about the price of bread, they also demanded that the royal bodyguards, the protectors of the king and queen, be disbanded at once. It might seem an odd demand, but the royal bodyguards had roughed up the crowds on previous occasions.

The crowd also demanded weapons of their own. And they were soon able to get them, as they surged into the city hall and laid siege to a stockpile of weapons. By this point, the women's march had been augmented by a large contingent of men. And this armed group of protesters next marched on the Palace of Versailles.

Marquis de Lafayette attempted to bring order to this chaos. Lafayette is an intriguing character in his own right, and we would be remiss not to speak of him in greater detail. He was born into a wealthy French family and became a commissioned officer when he was still a young teenager. At the outbreak of the American Revolutionary War in 1775, he decided to head to the American colonies and volunteer his services to the Americans.

His efforts were rewarded, and he ended up rising to the rank of general when he was just nineteen years old. After his return to France, he managed to get elected to the Estates General in 1789. Lafayette was a well-known and respected figure, and it was hoped that he would be able to somehow stem the tide of rebellion and bring back some sense of normalcy.

However, he soon became quite alarmed to find that many of his own troops were joining the maddened mob of protesters. Lafayette knew that he could not prevent the march. So, Lafayette made the decision to lead his troops in tandem with the mob as they marched to the Palace of Versailles. As Schama put it, this was done "to ensure that his soldiers were acting for, rather than against, the safety of the royal household."

Since Lafayette could not stop the march outright, he was positioning his reluctant men as shepherds of the protesters, hoping to at least provide enough damage control to prevent an all-out disaster at Versailles. He also made sure the palace was given advance notice of the mob headed its way by sending out a messenger on a fast horse to inform the palace authorities of what was transpiring.

King Louis XVI was actually out hunting when he was informed of the mob's impending arrival. He rushed back to the palace and began to brace himself for the breach. Crowds surged forward, and at one point, they very nearly reached the personal quarters of Marie Antoinette.

A soldier, either on purpose or by accident, had left a gate open. The protesters surged through the opening to gain access to the palace. The mob was heard shouting all kinds of insults toward the queen. Some even shouted that it would be necessary to "cut off her head" and even "fricassee her liver." The palace guard tried to stave them off even though they were entirely overwhelmed.

One guard whose name comes down to us as Monsieur des Huttes was stationed just outside the queen's chamber. He fired a shot into the crowd, hoping he might be able to disperse them. The shot hit one of the protesters. The shot did not cause the protestors to pause. Instead, it sent a fury through the throng, and they surged forward and seized hold of the guard. They supposedly killed this man on the spot.

Another guard by the name of Mimondre de Sainte-Marie tried to talk the crowd down. Once he realized he would be unsuccessful, he began shouting behind the barred doors he guarded. He screamed at the top of his lungs, "The Queen's life is in danger!" He shouted this fateful warning until the mob reached him and silenced him by ending his life.

However, before this man died, his words were heard by those inside, and evasive action was taken. The warning led Marie Antoinette to flee from her quarters, shouting for anyone and everyone who could hear her to help her make her exit. She was led through a secret passageway to the king's room. With nowhere else to go, she banged on the door in desperation.

It took several minutes, but finally, it was opened. The queen was reunited with her husband and her son and daughter, who were hiding inside with their retainers. The head of that brave guard who warned the queen of the threat she faced had his head placed on the tip of a long pike. The head was paraded around the palace grounds as a macabre kind of trophy.

By this time, Lafayette had made his way to the king's quarters and was able to take stock of the situation. Lafayette was flanked by members of the national guard, which had already shown their duplicity. He addressed these men and was able to convince them that he wasn't as bad as the mobs of Paris had let on.

In the French press, the king was blamed for every ill that the average person faced. And he was not only blamed; elaborate conspiracy theories were concocted to make it seem as if the king was intentionally inflicting harm upon the populace. After a crop failure in 1789, a rumor known as the "Famine Pact" went into circulation, declaring that the king and his cohorts were orchestrating an artificially engineered famine to deliberately destroy the peasantry of France.

As absurd as such conspiracy theories might sound, many in France did believe such things to be true. And as soon as one bought into such beliefs, it was no longer just a matter of a monarch who might have made some poor decisions. Instead, many were led to believe that the king was some sort of demonic tyrant hellbent on their own destruction.

Incredibly enough, though, Lafayette's efforts to convince the crowd were somehow successful, and the men who previously had trouble deciding their allegiance suddenly declared their unwavering support for the king of France. Feeling more secure, the king then decided to go to the balcony to address the mob himself. Incredibly, after all of the threats, insults, and deaths of the imperial guard, the crowd was receptive to the king and even showered him with a rousing round of cheers and applause.

You might be shocked to see the sudden change in how people viewed the king. Well, the bar is set pretty low when someone is seen as a monster. If someone has been thoroughly dehumanized and depicted as a horrible monster, it doesn't take much to surprise one's critics. Just a smile and a wave might be all that is necessary to dispel rumors that one is a hellhound with fangs and claws.

Once the king had their attention, he promised his subjects that he would do his best to end the bread crisis and to meet all of their many other concerns and demands. The king had been driven into a corner and was trying to use what was left of his power to instill faith in his people. And during that moment, he succeeded.

But his victory came at a cost. The crowd demanded that the royal family relocate to the French capital. The bullied and harried king felt as if he had no choice but to comply and agreed to leave the safety of his palace at Versailles and head into the thick of things in Paris. The king and his family were marched off to the French capital with the mob of protesters following close behind.

Some of the protestors had heads on pikes, which they gleefully and unabashedly waved in the air, but most simply had their coveted bread impaled on pikes instead. Yes, the giddy crowd, some with bread literally impaled on pikes, exulted in their triumph. Considering they had cornered and cowed the royal family into submitting to their demands, they were heard joyously chanting about how they now had "the baker, the baker's wife, and the baker's lad" in their possession.

However, having King Louis, Marie Antoinette, and their children would not solve all of their problems. Still, this vicious mob felt they had achieved some great feat. They seemed to think they would never go without bread again because they had the perceived producers of their sustenance in their possession. They would soon learn how wrong they were.

Chapter 3: The March toward a Constitutional Monarchy

"The most extravagant idea that can be born in the head of a political thinker is to believe that it suffices for people to enter, weapons in hand, among a foreign people and expect to have its laws and constitution embraced. No one loves armed missionaries; the first lesson of nature and prudence is to repulse them as enemies."

-Maximilien Robespierre

The next major step on the road to revolution was the dismantling of the Ancien Régime (Old Regime). First of all, the notion of France being based on the outdated practice of feudalism was addressed. The National Assembly met in early August to discuss measures for reform. The assembly ultimately decided to get rid of all forms of serfdom, feudal dues, and the tax privileges and exemptions of the elites. However, it must be noted that the National Assembly was not waving a magic wand to get rid of all the debts that were already owed. The intention was that people would continue to pay until these reforms took effect.

This situation back then would be akin to a presidential candidate in the United States today promising to do something just prior to an election to win votes. Many voters might conclude that a vote for this candidate would fulfill such a promise despite the fact that such a promise would take time to go into effect if it ever did.

A similar situation was afoot in France. French citizens were elated at the prospect of debt relief but did not understand the process that it involved. And due to this gross misunderstanding, many refused to pay prior to the reforms even taking effect. This made the financial crisis in France much more severe, as practically all payments ceased. The French government soon went bankrupt as a result.

Nevertheless, once the genie was out of the bottle, there was absolutely no way of putting it back. The peasants were armed, taxes had been absolved, and the old social order had been tossed out right along with it. The French Revolution had begun. But now that revolutionary reform was at hand, what was next? What would be the guiding principles of the revolution? To determine this, the French revolutionaries turned to leading French intellectuals to craft a bill of rights.

Everyone had seen the stunning success of the Americans' Declaration of Independence. The French sought to outdo the Americans with their Declaration of the Rights of Man and of the Citizen, which was made official on August 26th, 1789.

Although the Declaration of the Rights of Man and of the Citizen is often held up as the defining moment of the French Revolution, it was only meant to be a placeholder until a more definite constitution could take shape. The declaration stated that men had natural rights, including the right to life, liberty, and property. The rights declared in the document would influence the French Constitution, which was created a couple of years later, in 1791. There would be another revised constitution made in 1793.

Many are not aware, but a Founding Father of the United States—Thomas Jefferson—was behind the scenes when the Declaration of the Rights of Man and of the Citizen was made. Jefferson was serving in the capacity of a foreign minister on behalf of the US at the time. He was involved in reviewing drafts and was also behind the suggestion of providing a special provision that would enable future constitutional conventions to make amendments if necessary. Ostensibly, the groundwork was being laid for France to be a constitutional monarchy with King Louis XVI as the head.

Yet, paradoxically enough, France's quest for a constitutional monarchy would ultimately end with the French monarch being decapitated. It is a rather blunt way to sum it up yet entirely fitting for what occurred between the years of 1789 and 1792 in France. The first real step, as it pertained to the dismantling of the old order of the Ancien Régime, was the abolishment of feudalism, which occurred on August 4th, 1789.

Then, on August 11th, the revolutionaries decided to do away with the regular tithes requested by the Catholic Church. Instead of having parishioners give tithes to the church, the revolutionaries decided it would be better to have the church receive all funding from the state. But this was not done because the revolutionaries wanted to safeguard the finances of the church; rather, they wanted to have full control of the church.

If the state controlled the purse strings of the church, it would essentially control the church itself. The logic is simple enough. But what the ideologues underestimated was the fervent support the majority of the French people had for the Catholic Church, its institutions, and its traditions. Even if they arbitrarily decided to change the way things were done, it did not mean that everyone else would automatically follow suit.

They might have thought of the priests and nuns who filled up abbeys as nothing more than *faineants* (French for "do-nothings"), but that did not mean that the rest of the population agreed with them. Even so, the ideologues tried to push their luck and take their oppression of the church even further. On November 2nd, 1789, the National Assembly moved in favor of seizing church property and redistributing it as it saw fit.

Although communism was not yet a twinkle in Karl Marx's eye (considering he had not even been born yet), the French were falling back on what would become known as communist-styled principles. However, the worst was yet to come when, on July 12th, 1790, the National Assembly enacted the Civil Constitution of the Clergy, in which they sought to forever meld the functions of the church with civil law.

This move was a far cry from the separation of church and state that had developed in the United States. Instead, the French radicals sought to make the church a distinct arm of the state. They were not particularly religious. They just wished to bend the church to their own ends.

Members of the clergy were pressured to become mouthpieces for the revolution. In November 1790, the National Assembly made it clear to all clergy that if they did not make an official oath of submission to the government, they would be dismissed. Only about a quarter of the priests complied. Those in the more dominantly Catholic parts of France, such as Normandy, Brittany, and the Vendée, were the most steadfast in their resistance. The Catholic Church had much sway over the populations of these regions, and there was considerable pushback there against the French Revolution. The French state's reaction to this resistance was to crack down on the rebels. Priests who were deemed rebellious and contrary were punished, exiled, or even put to death.

It was in this backdrop of this turmoil that the political club of radicals known as the Jacobins came to prominence. The Jacobins were just one of many political clubs that had arrived on the scene. They had originated from a caucus within the Third Estate.

As mentioned before, France was broken up into three basic divisions of society. The First Estate was made up of the nobility. The Second Estate consisted of the clergy. And the Third Estate was made up of the vast bulk of the country, from the poorest of the poor to the more prosperous, non-noble shopkeepers and skilled artisans.

A French revolutionary ideologue named Abbé Sieyès made the most use of this state of affairs. He knew the Third Estate shouldered much of the national burden and that the people were upset. His political pamphlet titled "What is necessary that a nation should prosper?" pointed out the Third Estate was not just a separate class of French society but also the vast majority of the people and essentially the "nation itself."

He argued that since the true blood of the nation was in the Third Estate, who worked and toiled the hardest, the other two estates were nothing more than parasites sucking the Third Estate dry. This caricature of French society was portrayed by various illustrations of a poor and decrepit member of the Third Estate with a member of the clergy and a member of the nobility on their back.

This simplistic message of the Third Estate being forced to carry the load—the full burden of France's problems—truly resonated with the masses and became a lasting theme throughout the French Revolution.

Sieyès also argued that since the Third Estate represented the nation, then those outside of the Third Estate were not worthy of French citizenship. They were nothing more than corrupt, parasitical wasters of life and limb.

As Sieyès put it, "It is impossible to say what place the nobility and clergy ought to occupy in the social order. This is equivalent to asking what place should be assigned to a malignant disease which preys upon and tortures the body of a sick man."

The political clubs—especially the Jacobins—got quite a bit of mileage out of these stinging critiques of French society. The Jacobins thrived on this kind of rhetoric and sought to exploit it to the best of their advantage. They frequently met in a Dominican convent of the same name; thus, they became colloquially known as the Jacobins or the Jacobin Club.

By August of 1790, when the first reforms of the French Revolution were taking hold, the Jacobins of Paris numbered around 1,200. The Jacobins would meet on a regular basis in a building that used to be a church—that aforementioned Dominican convent—the Rue Saint-Honoré. It is ironic that the Jacobins met in a church for their meetings would later take on the form of a church function.

But instead of declaring the glories of God, those who stood before the podium expounded upon the rights of man. As the French were minimizing the role of their traditional Christian religion, they were seeking new solace in the quasi-religious philosophies of political clubs like the Jacobins. As we will see, the French intellectuals would use these philosophical movements as a replacement for religion and other traditions of the Old Regime.

Historian Simon Schama perhaps put it best when he described the Jacobin clubs as a mixture "between a church and a school." This is an apt description. The ideologues were doing their best to expound upon and teach their philosophies to those in attendance, and the insistence that all Jacobins adhere to those philosophical ideals became so intense and extreme that one could say that the members of the Jacobin Club became religious.

It has long been pointed out that human beings seem to have developed religion and philosophy for a reason. The second that one is thrown out, it is not long before it is replaced by another. The same thing occurred in communist Russia when the Christian Church was supplanted by a religious adherence to the communist ideal. For the most part, it seems that humans need something larger than themselves to focus on, whether it is a belief in an eternal, infinite God, the cult of communism, or the zealous implementation and adherence to revolutionary ideals. There is just an innate desire in us to follow something.

These political clubs were the first rudimentary efforts to provide the French mind and soul something they could latch onto in their search for meaning and self-discovery. The Jacobins were looking for something, but there were also those who were working under the nose of the French king who thought they could redirect the Jacobins toward embracing the French monarchy again. And Honoré-Gabriel Riqueti, Comte de (Count of) Mirabeau (more commonly just known as Mirabeau), was one of them.

Mirabeau was a deputy for the Third Estate. He represented the cities of Aix and Marseilles. During the first stage of the French Revolution, he rose to become a key figure in the French government.

Mirabeau is a complicated figure. Although he supported the establishment of a constitutional monarchy, he also insisted that the reforms that allowed for free speech, free press, and the like remain in place. Mirabeau supported the reforms, but he also wisely knew that once these rights were established, there would be no way to roll them back. At the same time, he advocated for the monarchy—even if it were a constitutional monarchy—to remain in place.

Mirabeau was a voice of pragmatic reason known for the rather gifted manner in which he could calm the nerves of agitated and angry crowds. On one occasion, he was able to talk sense into a crowd of agitated rioters in Marseilles. They were angry over the high prices of bread, but Mirabeau reminded them of how pointless their own actions were in the situation.

Addressing the angry mob directly, he reasoned, "Let us first consider bread. At the present time, dear friends, since wheat is expensive everywhere, how could it be cheap at Marseille?" It was a simple enough statement, but it brought some rationality back to the rioters. The whole country was facing high prices, so why did they feel the need to throw a fit over it? Mirabeau's simple logic seemed to sink in, and the rioters of Marseilles soon dispersed.

Mirabeau was a skilled navigator who often strode two worlds, with one foot in the royal palace working with the king and the other in the streets with the common people whom he claimed to champion.

As the tug of war between the king and the revolutionaries became more and more intense, Mirabeau suggested making some of the leading Jacobins members of the king's inner circle. In an apparent effort to reverse the old adage of "If you can't beat them, join them," Mirabeau was basically suggesting, "If you can't beat them, recruit them."

But he was not merely wanting to make nice with the Jacobins. He was wise enough to realize that once the Jacobin leadership was forced to deal with the problems of the French government firsthand—in other words, attempt to find solutions to the problems rather than just endlessly complain about them—they would understand that the issues facing the French were bigger than the monarchy and the political clubs. Mirabeau believed the Jacobins would have just as hard of a time solving them as the French government was having.

As Mirabeau sagely wrote, "The people have been promised more than can be promised; they have been given hopes that it will be impossible to realize. The expense of the new regime will actually be heavier than the old, and in the last analysis the people will judge the revolution by this fact alone—does it take more or less money? Are they better off? Do they have more work? And is that work better paid?"

In hearing Mirabeau's prediction of how the revolutionaries would be even worse administrators than the king's advisers, we can almost hear echoes of former US President Ronald Reagan's simple assessment, "Are you better off than you were four years ago?" Of course, Reagan was referring to a previous presidential administration, while the French were posed with the much more formidable task of assessing the wreckage and aftermath of their scrapping much of the former protocols of the Ancien Régime.

After the French shook off the previous constraints of absolute monarchy, they would have to ask that same question: were they better off? For many, the answer would be a clear and decisive no. Instead of having a better life, the French Revolution and its terrible aftermath would make the lives of many far worse than anyone could have imagined.

It is true that the noble ideals of the French Revolution would begin the framework of a more just and equal society, but it would take quite some time before they were actually put into practice. Ironically, the enlightened despotism of Napoleon Bonaparte would see some widescale implementations of the revolutionary reforms. Of course, he also looked out for his own best interest. For instance, he enforced slavery in French colonies after it had been abolished in 1794.

The Rights of Man and of the Citizen proclaimed the need for equality, freedom of speech, and representative government. And for a time, things looked promising. But ultimately, just about none of the declaration's promises were fulfilled. The whole notion of freedom of speech would become a joke since the French could not go against the ideals of the French Revolution; if they did, they might face arrest or even lose their head.

Mirabeau was perhaps more clear-headed than most since he was able to understand these ramifications before they played out. While others were gripped in revolutionary fervor and could not see much further than the tip of their nose, Mirabeau sagely understood what the end result of all of this tumult might be.

The monarch, King Louis XVI, would have very little to do with these reforms. In fact, King Louis attempted to escape the country in June 1791. These efforts were actually presaged by an earlier event that took place on April 18th, in which the couple was thwarted when they attempted to make a trip to St. Cloud. According to historian Simon Schama, it was on the Monday of Holy Week that the queen and king attempted to make a break for it.

They were blocked by an angry crowd, and once again, their own guard turned on them. An indignant Louis, who had just given in to many demands, declared his amazement that he, who had just granted such freedoms to the French people, was being denied his. The king was indeed a virtual prisoner, and even as he protested, his own guards hurled abuse at him. One even went as far as to call him a "fat pig" whose appetite was draining France's limited resources.

Ultimately, the king and his entourage had no choice but to give up their attempt to leave Paris and head back to their quarters. Yes, the baker, the baker's wife, and the baker's lad (not to mention the baker's daughter as well) were being held hostage by the French revolutionaries who refused to give them up. Nevertheless, knowing that escape just might be their only hope to get out of this ordeal alive, the royal family and their inner circle spent the next couple of months meticulously planning their next attempt.

This time, they would depart in the middle of the night under cover of darkness. In the king's and queen's eyes, it seemed that fleeing would be the only way they could restore their freedom and the monarchy. And just after midnight, on June 20th, 1791, the royal family, in full disguise, fled the Hôtel de Ville right under the nose of the unhelpful palace guards. They had their own royal detachments of troops shepherding them along the way, but even these men could not be entirely depended on. The royals didn't have much of a choice, though, and in this charged atmosphere of intrigue and animosity, just about everyone's sympathies were suspect.

Even worse, as they rode along in their carriage, local villagers began to recognize the king. Even though the king was in disguise, he was quite hard to miss since his face was printed on French currency. Ultimately, a local postmaster named Jean-Baptiste Drouet decided to call the king out, stopping the royal entourage in Sainte-Menehould and loudly proclaiming that the mystery guests were none other than the fleeing royals.

He actually rode ahead of the group and alerted local authorities. They were held in the town of Varennes at the mayor's residence, where they were made to await their arrest and transfer back to the capital.

After the king and queen were captured and returned to Paris, the façade of an all-powerful absolute monarch was finally dropped. It was hard for the people to trust the king as an authority figure after his embarrassing attempt to flee Paris in secret became known. As historian Simon Schama put it, this latest debacle only seemed to accomplish "the annihilation of the royal mystique." Whatever respect the king might have had left was lost after this failed attempt to flee. Eventually, King Louis and his wife, Marie Antoinette, were arrested and put on trial as traitors of the state.

Prior to their ultimate downfall, attempts were made to prop them up. On July 15th, 1791, the National Assembly decided to absolve the king of wrongdoing and go forward with plans to have King Louis made the head of a constitutional monarchy. However, this move created much anger, and soon a multitude of Parisians were out in force protesting.

On July 17th, protesters gathered at the grounds of Champ de Mars on the west side of Paris. Speeches were given, and petitions were signed, all denouncing the ruling that had been made. The demonstrations quickly got out of hand, and the National Guard was called out, with none other than the Marquis de Lafayette leading them. Lafayette was also accompanied by the mayor of Paris, Jean Sylvain Bailly.

Upon their arrival, the crowd almost immediately turned on the guardsmen. The increasingly agitated protesters shouted and hurled stones at the troops. At one point, one of the guardsmen fired his weapon. This action then set the ball in motion, and soon several of the troops were firing into the crowd.

Absolute pandemonium ensued as the demonstrators scattered. Once the smoke cleared, many lay dead. It has been estimated that as many as fifty of the protesters were killed, with many more wounded. Nevertheless, despite the ensuing backlash against this atrocity, the push toward the establishment of a constitutional monarchy went ahead as planned. And the First French Constitution would be put forward on September 3rd, 1791.

This is significant because it was the first effort made by the revolutionary government, under the auspices of the Legislative Assembly, to finalize the new proposed framework of French society in writing. This constitution was heavily influenced by the European Enlightenment and the American Revolution. However, many of the notions conceived within it already seemed somehow out of step with the rapid pace of events that were occurring on the ground.

The king was backed into a corner and forced to concede to virtually all demands. He even had his official title changed. According to this document, he was transformed from "King of France" to simply "King of the French." To the casual observer, this might not seem like that much of a difference. But it made all of the difference in the world.

When Louis was the "King of France," he was the absolute monarch whose rule was unquestioned. But as "King of the French," he had been rendered king only by the good graces of the French people, who allowed him to be king, not to lord it over them as a divine right but in order to safeguard the interests and will of the people.

So far, the turmoil of France had been contained within its borders, but it would soon spill out to affect the rest of the world. On January 17th, 1792, Austrian Emperor—and brother of Marie Antoinette—Leopold II issued demands for the French to leave territory they had seized in Alsace and to release the royal family from their house arrest. On February 7th, a formal alliance was made between Austria and Prussia.

The French issued counterdemands, asking the Austrians not to interfere with French affairs and respect the previous Treaty of Versailles of 1756. The Treaty of Versailles had made the French and Austrians allies, but this treaty had been forged during different times. Nevertheless, the French revolutionaries issued an ultimatum that Leopold II honor this treaty, giving him until March 1st to confirm his commitment to do so.

In one of the strange ironies of history, Leopold II abruptly passed away on March 1st, right before the deadline was set to expire. Leopold was succeeded by his son Francis. Francis would not honor the deadline imposed by the French any more than his father. His silence was interpreted to suggest his own intention for war.

In April 1792, the armed forces of France were sent to take on the forces of Prussia and Austria on the premise that some sort of counter-revolutionary alliance was being created to end the revolution. War was officially declared on Austria on April 20th, which led to Austria's ally Prussia declaring war on France that June. This group was known as the First Coalition.

Things would come to a head in July of 1792 when the Duke of Brunswick threw in his lot with the Austrians and led a Prussian force to invade French territory. This would lead to the seizure of the French city of Verdun on September 2nd. The next year would bring even more shocking developments for France. On January 21st, 1793, King Louis XVI was executed by guillotine.

Chapter 4: The Execution of Louis XVI and the First Republic

"Beware of letting yourselves be carried away by false pity. Your enemies will not spare you, if they have their way. No one abhors bloodshed more than I do, but if you do not want a veritable sea of blood, you must exact a few drops yourselves. To reconcile the public welfare with the needs of humanity, I propose that you decimate the counter-revolutionary members of the Commune, the magistrature, the departments and the National Assembly."

-Jean-Paul Marat

After war broke out with Austria and Prussia, the revolutionaries viewed the royal family as a liability at best and potential traitors at worst. This largely stemmed from the fact that the queen was related to the Austrian Crown, and it was believed that if the royals were not in direct cahoots with France's enemies, they were providing their enemies with an incentive to attack them.

This was seemingly all but proved when the commander of the Austro-Prussian forces, the Duke of Brunswick, fired off a manifesto on July 25th, 1792, in which he unequivocally stated that the forces at his command intended to intervene in France's affairs and forcefully restore the king's lawful authority. It also went as far as to warn that if the king and queen were in any way harmed, there would be widespread retribution.

Although this threat was issued in an effort to safeguard the royals, it had the opposite effect. Instead of taking care not to harm their hostages, the more radical revolutionaries took it as a reason to get rid of them. The Brunswick Manifesto only served to confirm the suspicions of the revolutionaries that the king and queen were liabilities that needed to be dispatched with posthaste.

On August 9th, the Legislative Assembly began to speak of dispatching the imprisoned monarch. But even though the king was in a poor position to fight back, getting rid of him would be no easy task. There were still many who feared and perhaps took the Duke of Brunswick's warning to heart that the repercussions of taking direct action against the king would be too great.

Nevertheless, the louder rabble-rousers were able to convince the assembly to act. After several hours of debate, it was determined that Louis would be put on trial. But the words of the delegates had to be matched with force. So, on August 10th, they sent out the Jacobin National Guard, which was augmented by mobs of rioters, to the Tuileries Palace, where the king was being guarded by 950 of his loyal Swiss Guards.

It is said that once the mob was at the gates of Tuileries, Queen Marie Antoinette was the most determined to make a last stand. She is said to have declared, "Better let ourselves be nailed to the walls of the Palace than to leave it." But her husband did not agree. Instead, he decided that in order to avoid more bloodshed, he should allow himself to be escorted to the assembly to answer the charges being leveled against him. As the king was led to the assembly, the mob turned on the Swiss Guards.

The Swiss Guard had loyally stood their ground, but upon receiving an order from the king, they returned to their barracks. As they attempted to stand down, the infuriated crowd moved in and began to literally shoot them in the back.

The king, the queen, and their children were imprisoned in a fortress called the Temple. This fortress was old even then and purportedly was used by none other than the Knights Templar (thus the name "Temple").

Perhaps it was a bad omen for those hauled inside its walls since the Templars had met a terrible fate when the French king decided to dispatch with them and disband their order in the 14th century. Behind the thick walls of the Temple, the king and queen were completely isolated and cut off from the outside world. All correspondence was forbidden, thereby ensuring that there would be no word as to their condition to friendly outside powers.

The surviving Swiss Guard were either imprisoned or killed in the streets. In September, gruesome events began. After rumors circulated that the prisoners were plotting to link up with an invading army, massacres broke out. Some prisoners were killed on the spot, while others were treated to a tribunal at the gates of the prison. If they were found guilty, which most were, they were walked out to be killed by the bloodthirsty mob that had gathered outside.

On September 21st, 1792, the assembly gathered to officially abolish the monarchy and declare the government a republic. Thus ended the farce of France's constitutional monarchy. Even the manner in which Louis was to be addressed had changed. He was no longer king; instead, he was called Louis Capet.

This name harkened back to Louis's ancestor, Hugh Capet, who became king in the year 987, starting what would be known as the Capetian line. King Louis XVI took offense to this perceived abrogation of his title, as it made him a citizen, not a king. When the mayor of Paris, Aubin Bigore du Chambon, addressed him as such, Louis indignantly replied, "I am not Louis Capet. My ancestors had that name, but I have never been called that."

In the meantime, the French war front received a significant and unexpected boon on September 20th when the French forces scored a decisive victory at the Battle of Valmy. The French, in many ways, viewed their stand at Valmy as their last stand. The Austrians had already descended like an avalanche, taking the towns of Longwy and Verdun. It seemed as if they were on a steady march to Paris itself.

As such, the French defenders viewed Valmy as their "Thermopylae." The battle was deemed a must-win in order to stop the approaching Austrians from reaching the French capital. Despite heavy French losses, the French lines held, and the Austrians were repulsed. This victory would indeed become a major turning point in the French Revolutionary Wars.

Incidentally, the famed German poet and playwright Johann Wolfgang von Goethe was traveling with the Austro-Prussian army and took note of just how demoralized the body of troops had become. It seemed that everyone at all levels knew what a colossal disaster Valmy was going to be. Goethe later recalled that since he was known as a wordsmith, it was requested of him to put words to what happened. Goethe could not help but proclaim, "From this place and this time forth commences a new era in world history, and you can all say that you were present at its birth."

One can only imagine what it would have been like if the French defenders had failed. Perhaps the Austrians would have marched on Paris. Perhaps the royal family would have been rescued by Marie Antoinette's former countrymen. But that was not how history played out.

Instead of Brunswick being able to make good on his threats of aggression, he was forced to order the troops under his command to pull back. The fate of the First Coalition would receive another blow on November 6th when they lost the Battle of Jemappes. The French got hold of a good chunk of what had been the Austrian-controlled Netherlands.

On that same fateful day of September 20th, 1792, the Legislative Assembly previously governing France was dissolved, and the National Convention was established in its place. The National Convention sought the complete removal of the French monarchy, which was officially done on September 21st. The new French Republic was declared on September 22nd.

The French royal family remained in prison with no hope of rescue on the horizon (the supposed rescuers were actually fleeing in the other direction). On January 17th, 1793, the former French king, Louis XVI, was found guilty of treason after a lengthy trial and handed a death sentence. Since all court proceedings were decided and rehearsed beforehand, this "trial" was for demonstrative purposes only. There was never any hope of the king being acquitted.

Nevertheless, the king's sentence was carried out on January 21st, 1793. Louis was awakened in the darkness of the early morning. After being allowed to have his last confession with his priest, he was then put in a carriage and driven off to the chopping block.

He asked beforehand that he be spared the indignity of having his hair cut off—a typical prerequisite of one who was about to have a giant blade cleave through their neck. But even this simple request was denied. After his hair was cut and final adjustments to the guillotine were made, the deposed king gave one last address to the crowd.

Staring out at the vast multitude that was eagerly awaiting his death, King Louis XVI declared, "I die innocent of all the crimes laid to my charge; I pardon those who have occasioned my death; and I pray to God that the blood you are going to shed may never be visited on France." The rest of the monarch's words were subsequently drowned out when drummers were ordered to furiously beat out a military march.

Those who were in charge of the toppled monarch's execution obviously did not want to give the king any chance to try and change the hearts and minds of the French populace. Resigned to his fate, King Louis XVI was directed to submit to the guillotine. With one quick pull of a cord and the even quicker hiss of a rapidly descending blade, the king's head was chopped clean off.

When King Louis XVI lost his head, the heads of state in the rest of Europe were appalled and horrified. They didn't want the revolutionary ideals to spread to their countries, especially if it meant losing their lives in the process. They were ready to go to war. France's National Convention anticipated as much and decided to preempt those foreign powers by making declarations of war on the Netherlands and Britain. Britain and the Netherlands reciprocated and were soon joined by others, principally Spain, Portugal, Tuscany, and Naples, which would all take part in the War of the First Coalition.

There were those in the French government who felt that external threats could be used to strengthen internal factions. The political faction known as the Girondins sought to unify French nationalistic feelings and sentiments during these calls for war. But instead of uniting the French in patriotic fervor, there were protests and even riots in Paris when attempts were made to establish a draft.

The radical group of French revolutionaries known as the Jacobins were largely in charge of the National Convention. The Jacobins had even less love for traditional institutions than their peers. In their efforts of radical transformation, they even went as far as to rename the months of the year and the days of the week. The week was also extended to ten days rather than seven. This was done in the hopes that it would obscure the traditional Christian Sunday by placing it in the middle of a full week of work and recreation.

Yes, atheistic and agnostic French elitists had seized control, and thinking they knew better than the French masses they claimed to champion, they sought to "cure" them of their religious superstition by completely subsuming and burying their impulses for it. Besides these absurd reforms, they also kicked off what would become known as the Reign of Terror, a time when they brutally persecuted anyone they perceived not to be on board with their agenda.

Ever since the storming of the Bastille, the French, regardless of their social class, were concerned with security and safety. The riotous mobs of the revolution never really died down, and spontaneous eruptions of animalistic rage seemed possible at any moment. This was the case in March 1793 when a mob of peasants rose up in the Vendée and launched a vicious assault on the local administration.

One eyewitness to these events, a seven-year-old boy named Germain Bethuis, later gave a disturbing account of what transpired that morning. Bethuis stated, "By now the sun had burnt off the mist to reveal a compact swarm of thousands of peasants, armed with pitchforks, skinning knives, billhooks, sickles, and more than a few hunting guns." As Germain remembered it, "Their wild cries alone were enough to spread terror."

Yes, it would be shocking for anyone to deal with a maddened mob of hundreds of angry, irrational, and hungry people. Even though attempts were made to reason with the crowd and meet some of their demands, they soon ran riot and began looting any targets associated with the local administrators. Even the clergy were not spared in this onslaught. A local priest by the name of Pierre Letort was cornered and viciously stabbed in the face multiple times.

But soon, France faced even more pressing issues than internal threats. France's foreign adversaries were poised to take advantage of France's internal turmoil. The most pressing problem was the threat of Austria. French troops were being demolished on battlefields in Louvain and in the Rhineland. The lack of central authority meant that any concerted action was often lost in a hopeless mire of bureaucratic bickering and inefficiency among the various factions leading the revolution.

Something had to be done to bring stability to this chaos. Henri-Maximin Isnard, who led the political club known as the Girondins, suggested the establishment of a committee that could see to the public's safety from both internal and external threats, the latter of which Isnard and his colleagues had expounded upon at great length in late 1791. In one exchange, Isnard went as far as to put France in the crosshairs of foreign aggression.

As Isnard put it, "The French have become the foremost people of the universe. So their conduct must now correspond to their new destiny. As slaves they were bold and great; are they to be timid and feeble now that they are free?"

Henri-Maximin Isnard and his colleagues were beginning to see their revolution not just as a localized French concern but also as one of great importance on the world stage. It was no longer enough to topple their absolute ruler. They also had to consider taking action against the other monarchs of Europe, such as those in Britain, Austria, and Russia.

The French Revolution was transforming into a crusade against absolutism itself, and the French revolutionaries began to see themselves at the center of this struggle for freedom. They began to feel they were engaged in a zero-sum game. Either they put the monarchs of Europe in their proper place, or they would be inevitably crushed by the foreign heads of state who were aligning against them.

Jacques Pierre Brissot, who was in attendance during these grave discussions, seconded this fear. As historian Schama put it, "Brissot sketched out the features of a vast conspiracy extending throughout Europe, designed to isolate and cripple French power forever. Posing a series of rhetorical questions, he put the pieces of the puzzle in place. Why had Russia suddenly made peace on its eastern frontier with Turkey if not to concentrate on something sinister? Why had the King of Sweden, a known correspondent of the Queen's since his visit to France in the 1780s, mobilized his armies? Why indeed had those arch-enemies Austria and Prussia fallen into each other's arms at Pillnitz? The answer to all these questions was a dagger pointing directly at the heart of the only truly free nation of men in the Old World."

The leading lights of the French Revolution could see the writing on the wall. They were weak at home and faced dire threats abroad since a vast coalition was forming against them. They needed to forge a special political body to tackle all of these threats. It was for this reason that the Committee of Public Safety was forged. This committee was officially established on April 6th, 1793.

The Committee of Public Safety, which was made up of twelve deputies, was given the power to direct the armed forces of France and govern the French nation. But its domestic investigations into the French citizenry and rooting out supposed internal enemies of the state would make this twelve-man committee infamous. The committee was tasked with keeping France "safe," and in the eyes of the revolutionaries, anyone who spoke out against the revolution was considered a danger to the state. The Committee of Public Safety considered itself to be the guardrail of the French Revolution. It was ready and willing to strike anyone who dared step out of line.

Jacobin firebrand Jean-Paul Marat had long been an unofficial mouthpiece of the Jacobin Club through his popular paper *L'Ami du*

Peuple or, as it translates into English, *The Friend of the People*. His paper became famous during the height of the French Revolution, as it launched brutal attacks on the king and queen of France, becoming the most popular vehicle of popular discontent. Marat himself was dubbed the "Friend of the People."

However, the Girondins did not appreciate Marat and felt that his hostile and often violent rhetoric was helpful, especially since he targeted fellow members of the revolutionary elite. The tensions in France were so high that the revolutionaries were more than ready to turn their wrath on each other. The political convention subsequently erupted into chaos, with Girondins like Marguerite-Élie Gaudet, Maximin Isnard, and François Buzot heaping their abuse upon the Jacobin leader.

In order to understand the Girondins' point of view, it is important to understand their origins and what they stood for. The Girondins first came about in 1791 during sessions of the Legislative Assembly. The group was forged by a prominent French lawyer named Jacques Pierre Brissot. Because of him, the Girondin faction was initially dubbed the "Brissotins." It was only later when it was noted that most of the membership of this faction hailed from Bordeaux, situated in what was known as the Gironde department, that the group came to be popularly recognized as the Girondins.

The Girondins advocated early on for an end to the absolute monarchy in favor of a republican government. Even so, they were considered moderates or at least far less radical than some of their Jacobin colleagues. The Girondins spoke at length of their desire for what they viewed to be a free France in which liberty and personal merit were of the utmost importance. And they viewed a republican government, with elected representatives, as the best system to ensure that these freedoms were protected.

At the same time, the Girondins cast a wary eye on their more radical colleagues in Paris who were calling not just for reform but also the leveling of French society. The Girondins sought a peaceful exit for the king—perhaps even clemency—whereas the more radical factions insisted the king must be killed. Since the king was eventually executed, the more moderate Girondin approach had clearly gone unheeded. Nevertheless, the Girondins continued to voice their concerns against the more radical mouthpieces at work in Paris, such as Jean-Paul Marat, whom his supporters had dubbed the "Friend of the People."

Just as a demonstration of how petty the barbs were, at one point, one of the fellow delegates at the convention quipped that the podium should "be disinfected after every speech by the Friend of the People." So, as much as we might want to assert that the politics of today are dire and extreme, all one has to do is look at the politics of the French Revolution, which took place well over two hundred years ago, and realize that politics has always been complicated. In fact, it was worse back then, as we will see with Marat's story.

Politics is often compared to a blood sport, and when adequate guardrails are not in place, things get out of control quickly. And in France in the 1790s, those guardrails were shattered. Gaudet was chirping that Marat was a "croaking toad," while Marat shouted that Gaudet was a "vile bird." As childish and juvenile as some of the exchanges sound, they were also dangerous since those slinging these barbs were angling to have their opponents not just mocked but also disgraced and possibly even killed.

Most importantly, the Girondins wished to get an indictment for Marat. They claimed he was inciting violence, and to prove their point, all they had to do was pull up his writings. Simon Schama described their tactics well when he stated, "The Girondins collected evidence from Marat's writings to show that he had violated the integrity of the Convention by calling for violent attacks on its membership."

These assertions led to a nineteen-page indictment, which was handed over to the Revolutionary Tribunal. This was a special court that had been created by the National Convention in March of 1793. It was specifically designed to try those who were dubbed to be enemies of the revolution. In other words, it tried those who were accused of engaging in counter-revolutionary activities.

The Girondins had essentially charged that Marat was stirring up violence and insurrection against the revolutionary government. As historian Simon Schama put it, "The Girondins collected evidence from Marat's writings to show that he had violated the integrity of the Convention by calling for violent attacks on its membership."

The inflammatory articles crafted by Marat in his newspaper were known for their over-the-top style and explosive language. Jean-Paul Marat, for his part, claimed that his words were being taken out of context and that not everything he said should be taken literally.

Of course, such things are open to interpretation. For example, Marat wrote of his "regret" over the fact that "a few hundred heads had been spared so as to preserve hundreds of thousands of innocents." Yes, his words can be literally interpreted as an advocation for violence here, but they can also be seen as rhetoric used to make a point.

At any rate, the indictment went forward, and Marat went to trial. But if the Girondins thought they had their arch-nemesis on the ropes, they were gravely mistaken. Rather than tarnish his image, the perceived political persecution of the stalwart Jacobin raised his profile and made him more popular than ever before.

When he appeared in court, he received a standing ovation. One can only imagine the shock and dismay of the Girondins to see the man they had targeted being showered with a spontaneous eruption of praise. And by the time Marat was given a chance to speak his peace, it was all but over. Marat's greatest gift was his words, and his defense was so brilliant and precise that even the Girondin-selected judges were swayed to take his side.

To the Girondins' chagrin, Marat was acquitted. Rather than going to prison or facing the guillotine, Marat left the courtroom a hero, and a veritable parade followed him through the streets. In celebration of Marat's acquittal, the Jacobins held a grand celebration on April 26th, in which it seemed that all of France was in attendance.

The Girondins had become increasingly unpopular. Their unpopularity was not helped when, in early May, they argued against price controls for grain. At this point, the political fortunes of the Girondins began to dim considerably. On May 16th, Isnard was made the head of the National Convention, and it was through his efforts that a last-ditch effort was made to turn the party's political fortunes around.

Maximin Isnard was radical in his approach, suggesting that a plot was underway to disband the National Convention outright. At one point, Isnard addressed the members of the National Convention and painted a rather dire picture of the future of France if such plots were not foiled. Isnard shouted out to those assembled, "I tell you, in the name of the whole of France, that if these endless insurrections should cause harm to the parliament of the nation, Paris will be annihilated, and men will search the banks of the Seine for signs of the city."

The Jacobins began to claim that the Girondins were responsible for a counter-revolutionary conspiracy. The Girondins were ultimately expelled from the National Convention and placed under house arrest, losing any influence they had left that June.

There was growing anger among those who felt politically excluded, and on June 13th, one of those took matters into her own hands. Her name was Charlotte Corday. She hailed from a family in the French region of Normandy. After the Girondins were disbanded, many Girondin exiles appeared in Normandy and spread the news of their alleged political persecution. Their accounts stirred up the hearts of many, and Corday was inspired to act. She sympathized with the Girondins, who tried to stop the violence from spreading. She traveled to Paris and tracked down Marat.

She arrived at his door on the morning of July 13th and demanded an audience with him. She lied, claiming that she had information about traitors in Normandy. Although she was turned away, Marat admitted her when she returned that evening. Marat gave her an audience while he soaked in the bath (he had a bad skin disorder). Corday gave him the names of Girondins but then plunged a knife into his chest. Hearing his screams, Marat's fiancé, Simonne Evrard, ran into the room. She placed her hand on the wound in an attempt to prevent his life's blood from pouring out.

However, it was no use. Charlotte Corday, in her unbridled rage, had struck home, plunging the knife into an artery, and Marat bled to death. This high-profile assassination ultimately played into the hands of the Jacobins, giving them more reason to institute harsh measures for the "safety" of the populace. The Friend of the People had been struck down, and now the Committee of Public Safety had to make sure that order was restored.

On July 27th, 1793, the firebrand Jacobin revolutionary Maximilien Robespierre was made a member of the committee. This group, which had been established for safety, would become the enforcers of the Reign of Terror since it was up to them to execute any decrees that were made by the National Convention.

Interestingly, Robespierre, a card-carrying Jacobin, was initially suspicious of the committee since it had been established by Isnard, who was a Girondin. Robespierre initially wondered if the committee was a bureaucratic power grab on the part of the Girondins. However, Robespierre would be seduced by the committee's ability to reestablish centralized control over official, state-sanctioned coercion, and he would become the unofficial head of it.

Writer and historian Simon Schama referred to this as nothing short of "the recapture of the state's monopoly of authorized violence." And that was precisely what the Committee of Public Safety sought to achieve. Ever since the toppling of the Ancien Régime and the fall of the king, just about all respect for state-sanctioned authority had been lost. The old regime had been dismantled, and there was no longer any respect for the old authority.

The Committee of Public Safety was attempting to assert itself as the new authority and the only legitimate government body to inflict state-sanctioned pain, suffering, and death on the populace if the committee members deemed it necessary to do so. Nation states must have law and order. But the nature of that law and order depends on who is pulling the levers of power.

If proper checks and balances are put into place, there should be some sense of justice and fairness involved in how law and order and the coercive measures of the state are applied. But if you have just a dozen or so cronies who have questionable intentions, motives, political persuasions, and objectives at the wheel, anything could happen. And that was precisely what happened in France.

Nevertheless, the committee knew that to become the supreme French authority, they had to deal with the murderous mobs the revolution had created. It was their job to roll back the very monsters they had created. And it is here that we see the first signs of a decisive split between the French intelligentsia and the protesters in the street.

These two combined elements had supplied the basic formula for the French Revolution in the first place. The intelligentsia provided the brains, and the violent mobs in the streets provided the brawn. This deadly combination, which had rioters with bread and bloody heads on pikes chanting the slogans of political pamphlets that had been written by the intelligentsia, brought the Ancien Régime to its knees.

But now, the intelligentsia was turning its gaze on the rebels in the street. The first sign that this change was in the works occurred the previous February, in 1792, when rioters, infuriated with rising prices at shops, stormed the markets. They did not always steal outright. Many of them actually paid what they thought were fair prices. However, these rioters had no idea that the shopkeepers were just as much a victim of high prices as they were.

The shopkeepers had to deal with the inflated prices of the wholesalers from whom they got their goods. And the fact that these rioters were paying the shopkeepers just a fraction of the inflated prices they had posted meant that the shopkeepers lost money and faced the risk of going out of business. The leading lights of the revolution knew the rioters were making things worse. Maximilien Robespierre was infuriated by the actions of the protesters, especially since their main concern was over what he derisively referred to as mere "paltry merchandise." The fact that he would dismiss the need of the hungry like this is a clear indication that Robespierre did not really care about the suffering of the French people. The starving masses just wanted bread to feed their families. This was not merely a desire for paltry merchandise—it was a desire for survival during extraordinarily difficult times.

Robespierre had no patience for the day-to-day concerns of the protesters in the street. He desired a complete overhaul of French society more than anything else. Many of the people who looted stores just wanted the price of bread to go down. They could have cared less about many of the "ideals" promoted by Robespierre and his ilk. They just wanted food to eat.

The intellectuals had once used their fury over high prices to get the masses to do their bidding. However, once the Ancien Régime had been undone, the intelligentsia could care less about petty concerns over—as Robespierre put it—paltry merchandise. And so, as previously mentioned, a committee was formed to help stop the protests over high prices, the very thing that had sparked the revolution in the first place. Those who really gave it any thought must have realized how ridiculous and absurd all of this was.

It was as absurd as it was duplicitous. The same intellectuals who were more than willing to bring down the hammer on the peasants were the same ones who had fanned the flames of revolution in the years prior. When the king and queen were in charge, pamphlet after pamphlet was gleefully fired off the presses, accusing shopkeepers and the Ancien Régime of price gouging or even a grand conspiracy to purposefully inflict famine.

It was all well in good to make such gross lies and exaggerations to ignite violence from the masses when the king was in charge, but when the revolutionaries were on top, they readily dispensed with nonsense about price gouging and plots since they knew that it was their own bottom line that was at stake. They knew that it was not price gouging that was causing the dire economic condition but rather rampant and out-of-control inflation.

The revolutionaries further realized they were no better prepared to fix the troubled economy than the Ancien Régime had been. But even so, they wanted the protesters to keep quiet and were prepared to muster all of the forces at their disposal to silence them. The irony of their situation was not entirely lost on the leading intellectual figures of the revolution, though.

Perhaps revolutionary figure and firebrand Louis Antoine Léon de Saint-Just summed it up best when he spoke of how "misery had given birth to the revolution" and that "misery could destroy it." It was decided that the passions that sparked the French Revolution—the very passions the intelligentsia had inflamed—needed to be extinguished.

Chapter 5: The Revolutionary Wars Heat Up

"The Revolution had been prepared by the most civilized classes of the nation and carried out by the most uncivilized and the roughest of people."

-Alexis de Tocqueville

The threat of outside intervention had been looming for some time. France had spent the better part of several years as a former monarchy rapidly unraveling into chaos. As much as the British might have initially looked upon the misfortune of their French rivals with glee, they were growing increasingly concerned, as were the Austrians.

As mentioned, French Queen Marie Antoinette hailed from Austrian royalty. The Austrian emperor, Leopold II, was her brother. Leopold II was concerned but cautious when it came to conflicts with France. However, after his abrupt passing, his son Francis, who succeeded him, proved to be much bolder.

It is debated whether or not this boldness can be attributed to Francis or his handlers. Scholars have argued that it was the advisers of the new monarch who pushed for war more than Francis did. And these advisers were supposedly emboldened further since they were receiving regular updates on French troop positions through regular correspondence with Marie Antoinette.

Yes, by the time the queen was put on trial for treason, there was some indication that the charges might have had some truth. But even so, one can't help but sympathize with the queen. Her husband had been killed, and she was being held as a prisoner by revolutionary forces. Who can blame her for trying to solicit aid from her family in Austria?

With this backdrop of political power play in place, the War of the First Coalition took shape. Initially, France appeared to be in quite a bit of trouble. On September 2nd, 1793, the French fleet was forced to surrender to British forces at the port city of Toulon. This was a stunning blow. France had an army but did not have a proper fleet.

The deficiencies of the French navy would be a lasting problem throughout the revolution, as well as the future Napoleonic Wars. The port city would be recaptured on December 15th, 1793, by General Napoleon Bonaparte himself. Napoleon was just twenty-four years old at the time, yet he was already a rising star in the French military. His efforts were indeed noted, and he was subsequently put in charge of the French artillery.

Napoleon next took part in a siege of British positions at Toulon's Fort de l'Eguillette. During this exchange, the daring young Napoleon put himself in harm's way time and time again. In one instance, a cannonball soared right past him. Although he was not hit, it was so close that the force of it zooming past him caused him to fall as if he had been struck. One can only imagine the astonishment of those under his charge to see Bonaparte jumping right back up after this near miss to take charge of his troops.

At the end of the day, Napoleon and his troops were able to storm the fortress and raise the French flag over Toulon once again. Napoleon also ingratiated himself with the Robespierres, getting well acquainted with Maximilien's brother Augustin in particular. But it was small consolation in the aftermath of the smashed French fleet, which was destroyed on December 18th, 1793.

As bad as this blow was, the French authorities received another internal one when the incredibly miserable and starving French peasantry appeared en masse at the Hôtel de Ville of Paris in September 1793, shouting their old familiar cry of "Bread! Bread! We need bread!"

One can almost imagine the distressing sight of this poor, starving, and entirely uninformed rabble dressed in rags and chanting almost zombie-like for something to eat. Such a situation could not be ignored. An authority of the French commune of Paris, Pierre Gaspard "Anaxagoras" Chaumette, sought to calm the frayed nerves of the populace by announcing that price controls would be put in place to lower the price of bread by the end of the week.

However, the people were not having it, and the protesters refused to disperse, demanding an immediate solution to the scarcity that they faced. Pierre Chaumette then attempted to position himself in a more sympathetic light, shouting out to those assembled, "Well, I too have been poor, and as a result, I know what it is to be poor! This is an open war of the rich against the poor; they want to crush us; well, we must prevent them. We must crush them ourselves; we have the strength to do so!"

Once again creating an imaginary enemy out of "the rich," Pierre Chaumette took a tactic out of the revolutionary playbook. Chaumette was well known for his attempts to create enemies where there were none. Just prior to King Louis XVI's execution, he famously declared that much of the problems the French faced were simply because the king was still alive, as if the mere fact that the monarch was still breathing was the sole reason for inflation, internal unrest, and the war clouds that loomed on the horizon.

But even with the king dead, the likes of Chaumette were still searching for enemies they could blame France's problems on. After bantering back and forth with the crowd in this manner, it was then suggested that the protesters return the following day on September 5th, when the National Convention next convened, so they could speak openly of their grievances.

The demonstrators decided to do that, and like clockwork, they appeared at the National Convention as suggested. But they were not going to wait for the speeches of delegates to wrap up. Instead, they barged right into the hall and began using brute force against those whom they were told were holding out on them. The Jacobins, who reigned supreme, were ready, though. With a newly retooled *armée révolutionnaire* ("army of the revolution"), they put down the demonstrators and instituted a crackdown that would become known as the Reign of Terror.

Chapter 6: A Revolutionary Terror in Their Midst

"You who sustain the vacillating country against the torrent of despotism and intrigue, you whom I know as I know God by your miracles, I address myself to you, monsieur, to beg you to join with me in saving my poor region. I don't know you but you are a great man. You are not merely the deputy of a province; you are the representative of humanity and the republic."

-Louis Antoine Saint-Just

The start of the so-called "Reign of Terror" would leave countless dead and imprisoned. Although some scholars disagree on the start date of the Reign of Terror, most agree that it began with a Jacobin-inspired crackdown that was instituted on September 5th, 1793. Although no one knows the exact number, historians estimate that tens of thousands perished during this terrible episode in French history.

Its end can be definitively stated since it is generally agreed that it came to an end when its architect, Maximilien Robespierre, and his cronies became its last victims. Robespierre faced his own execution on July 28th, 1794. But a whole lot occurred in those nearly eleven fateful months of oppression. The first major milestone was when the Law of Suspects was issued on September 29th, 1793.

This legislation set down the exact procedures for rooting out supposed enemies of the state into French law. This set in motion a nationwide program of surveillance in which anyone who was deemed to be subversive was rounded up and arrested. Yes, ironically enough, as much as pre-revolutionary French philosophers had railed against the Spanish, Portuguese, and Roman inquisitions, the successors of the French Revolution decided it was high time to institute one of their own.

It is said that during this period, hundreds of thousands—some estimate roughly around 500,000—were placed under arrest. The fact that anyone could be arrested for just about any reason was an obvious departure from the supposed lofty goals of the French Revolution and the freedoms that were explicitly mentioned in the Declaration of the Rights of Man and of the Citizen.

Nevertheless, Jacobin leader Maximilien Robespierre had no problem with using force to secure his vision of France's future. He had no qualms about hauling supposed suspects before tribunals on the flimsiest of charges. As Robespierre himself put it at the time, "Public notoriety accuses a citizen of crimes of which no written proofs exist, but whose proof is in the heart of all indignant citizens."

What does that mean? Robespierre, with his chillingly cryptic words, is basically stating that there does not need to be any real, legal proof that a crime exists as long as someone has been deemed to be at odds with the heart of the revolution. If a person was believed to be subversive to the ideals of the revolution, they could expect wrath that poured from, as Robespierre put it, "the heart of all indignant citizens."

It truly is a chilling thing to contemplate. The Reign of Terror began as a coercive crackdown against riotous protests over the price of bread. However, most of those rounded up during this period were suspected of directly plotting against the revolutionary government. Religion sometimes played a role since Christianity was actively suppressed. Christianity came to be viewed as being potentially subversive, so outward showings of one's faith could land one into a lot of trouble with the revolutionaries. According to writer and historian Ian Davidson, if one was caught openly displaying a crucifix, they could be hauled in for questioning.

French society saw the complete breakdown of trust between friends and neighbors. As is always the case, when society is forced to look inward for "enemies," friends, neighbors, and even family members begin to turn against each other, with old grievances being settled under the guise of something larger than themselves. In the case of France in the 1790s, that larger thing was revolutionary fervor.

Esteemed French scholar and historian Jules Michelet openly admitted the Jacobins were the "thought police of the revolution." As Michelet put it, "It was not a small matter to be excluded from the Jacobins. This formidable society, while keeping the form of a club, was in reality a grand jury of accusers. Its membership list was the book of life or death."

One person who most certainly did not fit into this revolutionary club was the former French queen, Marie Antoinette. Perhaps the most hated focal point of the revolution, she managed to outlive her husband, who had been executed by way of the guillotine in January 1793. However, Marie's life would not last for long, as the thought police of the revolution found a way to bring her down as well. Immediately after her husband was killed, Marie Antoinette was placed under guard at the prison palace of the Temple.

It was hoped that the former French queen could remain out of sight and out of mind as far as the French people were concerned. However, during the summer of 1793, her handlers were shocked to find that word had been spreading of how tenderly the queen had been treating her two children—her surviving daughter and son—from their quarters in the Temple.

As absurd as it might sound, Marie Antoinette's handlers became alarmed that their dehumanization of the former royal would backfire. They feared that if the news became widespread, with people gossiping in the street that the queen was a caring and selfless mother, all of the great pains taken to paint her as a terrible monster might amount to nothing. After all, it is hard to vilify a person who is kind.

To stop the gossip from continuing, Marie Antoinette's seven-year-old son, Louis Charles, was ripped from her side. The boy was transferred to a cell below the queen's quarters, where she could hear his wretched sobs but do absolutely nothing to comfort him. Poor Louis would perish, locked away in his room, in 1795. He would have been only ten years old.

Marie Antoinette was ultimately hauled before the tribunal on October 14th, 1793. She was—predictably enough—tried for treason. She had much of the same old, recycled charges leveled at her, which used her ancestral roots to Austria to suggest that she was in cahoots with the Austrian government, with whom France was currently at war.

Despite the gravity of the situation and considering what she had already been through with the execution of her husband and all of the other deprivations that had been foisted upon her, she handled herself well. She denied her enemies the pleasure of seeing her grovel before them, as it is said that she stood tall and answered all the questions given to her with a firm and confident tone of voice.

She denied any wrongdoing and insisted that the happiness of the French people was always her and her husband's number one goal. Nevertheless, she was found guilty and would ultimately lose her head by way of the guillotine on October 16th, 1793. The morning prior to her execution, Marie Antoinette managed to write one last note to her sister-in-law Elisabeth.

The letter begins:

"It is to you, my sister, that I write for the last time. I have just been condemned, not a shameful death, for such is only for criminals, but to go and rejoin your brother."

The condemned queen is, of course, referring to her husband, who had already been guillotined. She reminds her sister-in-law Elisabeth that no matter what anyone might say, she could see through the condemnation that has been heaped upon them. Even though the two royals received the harshest of penalties, she did not see herself and her husband as being the same as criminals worthy of a shameful death.

She goes on to further stress her stance by stating, "Innocent like him, I hope to show the same firmness in my last moments. I am calm, as one is when one's conscience reproaches one with nothing."

Here, the queen again insists that her conscience is clear. It is true that the queen was unfairly targeted from the very start of her reign, but the fact that she refuses to even acknowledge that any mistakes might have been made on the part of the royals is a departure from King Louis XVI's reaction. Although King Louis thought that he and his wife had been unfairly targeted and dehumanized by the intelligentsia, he was willing to acknowledge his past mistakes.

Marie Antoinette's greatest concern was always for her children, whom she knew would have to live the rest of their lives (no matter how short they might be) without either of their parents. It was to this end that she implored her sister-in-law, Elisabeth, "who out of love have sacrificed everything to be with us," to look after the welfare of her two surviving children.

Her son, as previously mentioned, perished in his prison cell in 1795. It is hard to know what troubles he faced, although it does seem he was treated with some respect. However, during his autopsy, his body had marks all over it, as if he had been beaten. Marie Antoinette's daughter, Marie-Thérèse, would survive the Reign of Terror. She was released from captivity on December 18th, 1795, and she headed to Vienna, where she knew she would be welcomed.

Marie Antoinette then goes on to add, "I have learned from the proceedings at my trial that my daughter was separated from you. Alas! Poor child; I do not venture to write to her; she would not receive my letter. I do not even know whether this will reach you."

The queen was right to assume this, as her final missive did not actually reach its target. Elisabeth never even knew the letter existed. She would be sentenced to death by the guillotine in May 1794.

Marie Antoinette's letter goes on, with the queen hoping that her surviving son and daughter would learn to support each other through the many sorrows, trials, and tribulations that they would likely face in the aftermath of her demise.

The doomed queen advised, "Let them, in short, both feel that, in whatever positions they may be placed, they will never be truly happy but through their union. Let them follow our example. In our own misfortunes how much comfort has our affection for one another afforded us! And, in times of happiness, we have enjoyed that doubly from being able to share it with a friend; and where can one find friends more tender and more united than in one's own family?"

In the letter, Queen Marie Antoinette then turns her attention toward her son. She asks Elisabeth to make sure that the child keeps his father in his memory but also warns against him having any notion of seeking out vengeance.

She writes, "Let my son never forget the last words of his father, which I repeat emphatically; let him never seek to avenge our deaths."

It is thought-provoking to consider these final few words of the queen. Here, she is strongly suggesting that her son should not seek any vengeance against her and her husband's persecutors. It is perhaps a bit difficult to get inside the mind of this condemned monarch, but one must wonder if she was envisioning a future in which the monarchy was restored and her son was at its head. Did she imagine her son sitting on the throne as an adult and contemplating how he would exact vengeance against those who had wronged his parents?

In some ways, due to the incessant negative portrayals of Marie Antoinette by her detractors and some of her own statements, it is hard to imagine her wishing such magnanimity upon those who persecuted her and her family. But in one of her last moments of life, she seemed to believe that her son should show mercy and restraint should he live to take power over France.

Perhaps Marie Antoinette was influenced by Christian teachings on mercy and forgiveness. But perhaps she was wise enough to know that a cycle of retribution would not bode well for any monarchy. And history would ultimately bear this out when the monarchy was later restored under Louis XVI's brother, Louis XVIII.

Louis XVIII found that it was best to forgive and forget the terrible trespasses that had occurred as quickly as possible. Just as Marie Antoinette had stated in her final letter, it seemed that the only way to get out of the terrible cycle of hatred, grievance, and retribution that France had found itself in was to forgive, forget, and move on as much as was feasibly possible.

We can't forget, of course, that in these final words of Marie Antoinette, we see not just the last words of a monarch but also the pleas of a worried mother. Although the stoic queen was resigned to her own fate, she was deeply distressed over what might happen to her children. We get some indication of family discord with the queen's son as she urges her sister-in-law to be patient with the child, who apparently had caused some previous distress.

Marie Antoinette ends her missive, saying, "Farewell, my good and tender sister. May this letter reach you. Think always of me; I embrace you with all my heart, as I do my poor dear children. My God, how heart-rending it is to leave them forever! Farewell! Farewell!"

The letter did not reach Elisabeth; instead, it was seized by the prosecutor, Antoine Quentin Fouquier-Tinville, and then stashed away with his personal belongings. Although the note did not reach its intended target, it became an unexpected treasure for historians later on, marking the last moments prior to the former queen of France's demise.

At any rate, shortly after these last few heartfelt words were penned, Marie Antoinette was marched to the guillotine to meet her untimely end. She was hauled out of her jail cell around seven in the morning and placed inside an open carriage (some describe it as more of a cart), where she was completely exposed to the elements, including anything the crowds might throw at her. To make matters worse, her transport was purposefully stopped on more than one occasion so that her handlers could point her out to the crowd.

During these moments, seething throngs of Marie Antoinette's former subjects mocked and hurled all kind of vile words and cruel taunts her way. Nevertheless, it is said that she remained stoic and strong and did not stoop to their level. Instead of shouting down the abusive mob, she was heard mouthing prayers to God. Although this was meant to be the execution of a former monarch, in many ways, Marie Antoinette took on the guise of a martyr.

The death of Marie Antoinette was just as dramatic as the saints of old being led to burn at the stake or being thrown to the lions. The procession to the guillotine was a major ordeal, and it was already the middle of the day by the time the former queen reached her destination. Stoic and refined until the end, it is said that her last words came about when she accidentally stepped on her executioner's foot. She was heard telling him, "Excuse me, sir, I did not do it on purpose."

It was as if Marie Antoinette was resigned to her fate and determined to stand in stark contrast to the bloodthirsty mob that howled for her demise. Unlike those who clamored for her death, she wanted to make it absolutely clear that she had no rancor within her. As the guillotine dropped, she remained quiet. And without any sign of protest, the life of the queen had been snuffed out.

Even more pivotal for the course of the revolution was what happened a couple of weeks later. On October 31st, twenty-one leaders of the disgraced and demobilized Girondins were executed. The pretense of any sense of justice was not even bothered with at this point. According to French historian Michelet, "There was no hypocrisy in the trial. Everybody saw right away that it was just about killing. They disregarded all formalities still customary at this period in the Tribunal revolutionaries. No documents were produced. There were no lawyers for the defense. Several of the accused were not allowed to speak."

The propaganda of the intellectual elite had fallen flat. Even the simplest of simpletons could see that the wool was being pulled over their eyes and that the elitists had blood on their hands. There was no way to sugarcoat the fact that blood lust was being engaged on an official level through the organs of the state.

Show trials are all about trotting folks out and publicly condemning them without any hope of recourse or defense. And that is what happened to these condemned former leaders of the Girondins. Yes, it was a grisly

Halloween in 1793, as the last vestiges of the Girondins were ground under the heel of the Jacobin boot.

It is worth noting that the first French Constitution had already been scrapped at this point in favor of another constitution, which was partially drafted by the leading Jacobin architect of the Reign of Terror, Maximilien Robespierre. This new constitution was formally adopted in June of 1793. The supposed constitutional monarchy of the first constitution became null and void after the king lost his head. So, Robespierre's obvious impetus was to forge a constitution that did not have any need for a monarch to be involved.

Besides abrogating the need for the monarchy, the document also greatly expanded upon the original virtues declared in the Declaration of the Rights of Man and of the Citizen. In particular, it sought to ensure things like popular sovereignty, the right of association, and the right to resist oppression. The right to resist oppression was the vaguest of these supposed rights. Just how does one define oppression? And how could one say that they weren't being oppressed at the time? After all, the Reign of Terror was in full swing, with multiple fingers pointing in multiple directions at multiple oppressors, both real and imagined.

The Jacobin-backed Reign of Terror was so wide-reaching that by December of that year, more than fifty detention centers were in operation in Paris alone. And by that December, they contained some seventy thousand souls between them. The people who were arrested and executed included men and women, both rich and poor and obscure and prominent.

One of the highest-ranking prisoners was Louis Philippe II, Duke of Orléans. He was known to be the most affluent figure in all of France and had once been an elected representative in the National Convention. He was also a cousin of the former king, whom he had actually voted to have executed. Louis Philippe was arrested simply because his son proved treacherous to the revolutionary cause when he fled to enemy lines and switched sides.

His son—the Duke of Chartres—had become quite disgusted with his father when he voted to have King Louis XVI executed. Having had enough of the revolutionary fervor that gripped France, he decided to defect to the Austrians, taking up refuge with them and fighting for them. This would prove to be ironic since just prior to his son making this fateful decision, Louis Philippe II, Duke of Orleans, in his capacity as a representative of the National Convention, had voted to approve a protocol that stated anyone viewed to be even the slightest bit complicit with a defector became a suspect by default.

Louis Philippe II was found guilty by association, and that was more than enough for the revolution to suspect him. Louis Phillippe was known for having a great sense of humor, and he apparently took it all in stride. Noting the absurdity of it all, just prior to his execution, he is said to have remarked, "Really? This seems a bit of a joke."

However, not everyone was laughing. Some leading lights of the revolution did try and put the brakes on the Reign of Terror. For instance, on December 5th, 1793, Camille Desmoulins published a pamphlet called *Le Vieux Cordelier*, which called for an end to the persecution. In another issue that was released on December 17th, 1793, Camille Desmoulins was bold enough to directly call for an end to the Reign of Terror.

Robespierre initially took a surprisingly conciliatory tone to these attacks on the methodology of the Reign of Terror. On December 20th, he proposed to set up a committee of justice, which would reexamine some of those being held under suspicion. This conciliatory and tame response only emboldened Desmoulins further. In his next publication on December 24th, he demanded that the prisoners be immediately released.

He declared, "Unlock the prisons for the 200,000 citizens whom you call suspects, because, in the Declaration of Rights, there are no houses of suspicion. You want to exterminate all your enemies by the guillotine! But was there ever a greater madness? Believe me, liberty would be strengthened and Europe conquered if you had a Committee of Clemency!"

Still, Maximilien Robespierre showed unusual restraint when dealing with the fired-up Desmoulins. Robespierre even waved off the suggestion of expelling him from the Jacobin Club. Instead, he stated that he would merely destroy his publications. However, Robespierre's tolerance would not last forever, and Desmoulins, along with several other dissenters, were rounded up and arrested. Camille Desmoulins would be given a farce of a trial just prior to his execution on April 5th, 1794.

And shortly thereafter, the French Revolution did indeed devolve into what seemed to be complete and utter nonsense. In the spring of 1794, Robespierre, seeking to keep up the revolutionary fervor of the populace, began to create what can only be described as a religious cult. Ever since the beginning of the French Revolution, there were many who wished to dismantle Christianity and replace it with a new religion.

Many of the leading lights of the revolution were deists who believed in a higher power while having great disdain for organized religion. These sentiments were echoed in the fact that the French Constitution mentioned a "supreme being" but did not go as far as to specify what that supreme being might be. Robespierre felt the need to fill the void that the suppression of Christianity had created, so he began to create his own religion, placing himself at the head.

He led religious processions and had people sing their own improvised hymns in which they sang not praises to God but to the glories of the revolution and their detestation of monarchs. As ridiculous as it all sounds, there were plenty of poor, disillusioned French who fell into the cult.

Robespierre's colleagues were not pleased with these developments and secretly despised his efforts. Robespierre's cult was more a cult of personality than anything else, and as soon as he was dispatched, his experimental religion would fall by the wayside as well.

The Reign of Terror was running out of steam, and neither it nor a new religion for the masses would bolster the fortunes of Robespierre and his Jacobin colleagues.

Nevertheless, Robespierre sought to involve all aspects of the lives of the common French with his new cult. The culmination of all of this religion was an extravagant production that Robespierre put together on June 20th, which was referred to as the Festival of the Supreme Being.

During Robespierre's invocation at this event, he proclaimed, "The true priest of the Supreme Being is Nature itself; its temple is the universe; its religion virtue; its festivals the joy of a great people assembled under its eyes to tie the sweet knot of universal fraternity and to present before it [Nature] the homage of pure and feeling [sensible] hearts."

Using themes, symbolism, and words that he felt would resonate with the French people, Robespierre was trying to stir the hearts and minds of the masses. He was trying to get a reaction. But he did not expect the reaction that he ultimately received.

Chapter 7: The Thermidorian Reaction and the Directory

"It has been said that terror is the principle of despotic government. Does your government therefore resemble despotism? Yes, as the sword that gleams in the hands of heroes of liberty resembles that with which the henchmen of tyranny are armed. The government of the revolution is liberty's despotism against tyranny."

-Maximilien Robespierre

Robespierre desperately sought to transform the face of French society. He renamed the month of July as "Thermidor." And in the month of Thermidor, his opponents moved against him in what has been subsequently dubbed the "Thermidorian Reaction." The term "Thermidorian" is a historically vague one. Anyone who opposed Robespierre and the direction in which he was leading France fell into this catch-all category.

Some of the opposition were against Robespierre on a purely ideological level, while others might have had personal vendettas against Robespierre or were acting out of fear. Some who had gotten on Robespierre's bad side might have felt that taking out Robespierre would be the only way to avoid losing their own head.

On a very basic level, the Thermidorians were those who believed Robespierre had overstepped his bounds and were seeking to curtail the abuses that this enlightened madman had unleashed. As a result, Robespierre and his fellow Jacobins were thoroughly denounced.

Robespierre would be cornered, and during an attempt to arrest him, he would try his hand at suicide.

The effort failed, and he ended up with a shattered jaw instead. Robespierre was seized while in this terrible state and put on trial. One more sham trial later, and he would be marched off to the guillotine. The bandage covering his jaw was deemed to be too much of a distraction, so it was forcibly ripped off of him. And unless an animal howl of pain counts, Robespierre, the great orator, did not have any last words. He howled in pain, the blade went down, and he was gone.

However, the tumult was not yet over, and the Thermidorian Reaction would continue. Southern France, in particular, would see spontaneous eruptions of violence against Jacobins. One must realize that southern France was staunchly Catholic, and much of its reaction can be traced back to the way the Jacobins tried to suppress the Catholic Church.

Also, during this reactionary wave, former political opponents of Robespierre and the Jacobins were released from prison. The Girondins were put back in power. This led to a renewed spate of retribution, this time aimed at the Jacobins and their supporters. Some of this retribution was on the official level, with Jacobins being arrested and detained, but much of the rest of it took place in the streets in the form of spontaneous eruptions of reactionary, mob violence of the worst kind. After all, there were many scores to be settled.

The Thermidorians created even more trouble by removing the price controls the Jacobin administration had instituted to get the rising cost of food under control. This led to renewed shortages, and once again, the average French citizen was in a desperate state of affairs. Their desperation led to what has been cited as the last major protest of the French Revolution.

On May 20th, 1795, a huge mob of French protesters stormed into a political convention that was being held among the Thermidorians. Just prior to this protest, legislation was passed that gave representatives of the Thermidorian government sweeping authoritarian power, allowing them to arrest and disarm any rabble-rousers as they saw fit.

Dismissing any previous notions of the citizenry having the right to protest, the elites who wielded power had little time or pity for the commoners and used martial force to dispel and disperse them. In the aftermath of this dispersal, the Directory was created on June 21st, 1795. The Thermidorian reactionaries were determined not to be swayed by the previous radical reforms of the Jacobins and insisted on a more conservative constitution.

The Directory was basically a legislative body made up of two houses: the Council of Ancients and the Council of 500. The Council of Ancients was the upper chamber, which had the authority to approve or reject legislation proposed by the lower chamber, known as the Council of 500. The Council of Ancients did not propose new legislation themselves, but it was up to its members to approve governmental reforms.

At the top of this structure was an executive branch, a board of five directors. These five directors consisted of well-known members of the revolutionary elite: Paul Barras, Louis Marie de La Révellière-Lépeaux, Jean-François Rewbell, Étienne-François-Louis-Honoré Letourneur, and Lazare Carnot.

The makeup of the Directory was fairly ingenious and had the potential for some much-needed checks and balances in the French legislature. Members were put in place through an indirect method of specially designated electors. The governing council was meant to be held accountable by the legislature.

It is important to note that as much as the French Revolution was inspired by the American Revolution, the major difference was that the American Founding Fathers focused on employing checks and balances between governmental bodies, whereas the French, with their political clubs routinely vying to monopolize all power, dangerously lacked any checks to prevent authoritarian abuse. Still, the Directory was just a fledgling enterprise at its outset and was in danger of dissolving from the beginning.

And from its very inception, there were plots and counterplots in the works between various political factions. One of the most infamous dissenters of the Directory was François-Noël Babeuf. Babeuf was known for his left-wing ideology and was a known agitator in France. He was briefly imprisoned in 1790, and upon his release, he began to work on a firebrand periodical to spread his views.

In the *Correspondant Picard*, Babeuf wrote about his ideas on agrarian reform. With echoes of the future ethos of communism, he insisted that there should be a general redistribution of land. Babeuf believed the wealth earned by others needed to be gathered up and redistributed to the masses. He disregarded the virtues of hard work and merit and sought to forcibly achieve economic equality through forcible redistribution.

At the height of the Reign of Terror, in the spring of 1793, Babeuf was once again arrested, only to be released in July 1794 after the architect of the terror, Robespierre, was arrested. Ironically, Babeuf came to prominence again during the reactionary wave of the Thermidorians. In the Thermidorians' mad rush to reverse course and undo everything the Jacobins had done, they practically dumped all of the prisoners arrested by the Jacobin regime onto the street.

But although Babeuf was no friend of the Jacobins, he would soon prove himself to be a thorn in the side of the Directory. After he began to openly deride the efforts of the Thermidorians, he was again placed into custody on February 12th, 1795. He would not stop, and even after he was released, he continued to make plans for overthrowing the Directory so that he could institute his own plans for the redistribution of wealth.

This time around, he was able to pull many disgruntled Jacobins into his orbit. With this new political coalition, Babeuf began speaking about a renewed push for revolution in November 1795. Babeuf's efforts would ultimately be defeated, and he would be again arrested in May 1796. This was ultimately the end of the road for Babeuf, who was subsequently tried for treason, found guilty, and executed the following year.

The driving force behind the Directory was a French general named Paul Barras. He was actually a close associate of Napoleon Bonaparte. Barras would open the door for Napoleon's eventual entrance into executive leadership.

Initially, the Directory did not fare well, and as the political body of France once again went into a fit of convulsions, France faced a wave of counterrevolutionary activity that threatened to pull the rug right out from under the Directory.

Coincidentally enough, Bonaparte and the troops at his command were able to prevent the Directory's complete collapse. As the general's compound was being targeted, Napoleon strategically positioned artillery around it to ensure that it was not stormed. Under Napoleon's watch, there would not be another storming of the Bastille. In fact, these efforts could be viewed as France's first steps in its long march toward authoritarianism.

But paradoxically enough, these efforts led to Napoleon being heralded as a savior of the republic. For his efforts, he was made the commander of the Army of the Interior. Napoleon essentially declared martial law and was able to go from house to house taking weapons. Since the revolution and unrest had begun with the storming of the Bastille and the seizure of arms, Napoleon realized that the only way to have order would be to take those arms back.

Interestingly enough, while he was in the midst of this search, he met a kid named Eugène de Beauharnais. One of Napoleon's men was attempting to take a sword from twelve-year-old Eugène, but the child begged him not to take it since it had belonged to his deceased father. The young man confronted Napoleon and declared that he would end his own life if the sword was not returned at once.

Napoleon felt sorry for this kid and relented. Despite his own instructions to seize all weapons, he made an exception for Eugène. Napoleon would meet the boy's mother, Joséphine, a short time later, and the two would almost immediately hit it off. Joséphine would become Napoleon's first wife, with the two becoming wed on March 9th, 1796. Although Napoleon was not a central figure in the French Revolution at its beginning, he would take a leading role later.

From the perspective of France's foes, their main objective was to contain the turmoil of France and make sure its problems did not spill over into neighboring regions. For Austria, its role and objectives were far more personal. The queen of France, who hailed from Austrian royalty, had been executed. Austria was also in steep debt due to the War of the First Coalition.

Austria was more determined than other nations to settle the score with France. Austria had technically been at war with France ever since 1792, and it was the one with the most to lose should it fail. And it was determined to come out on top. Ever since hostilities had erupted in that fateful year of 1792, the disputed Piedmont region of northern Italy had served as the main battleground. Napoleon rolled the dice by throwing the vast bulk of his troops at the Austrian armies encamped in Piedmont near the Alpine region of France.

Initially, it seemed as if the French were destined to lose. Beaten and battered from previous conflicts, they were almost entirely unprepared. There was a dire lack of equipment, and many of the French troops lacked proper footwear, trekking the snowy mountains practically barefoot.

Napoleon addressed these needs just prior to the battle. Bonaparte is said to have proclaimed, "Soldiers, you are insufficiently clothed, malnourished; the government owes you much but is unable to repay anything. I wish to lead you into the most fertile valleys of the world. Wealthy regions, large cities will be under your power. You will find in those parts honor, glory, and riches." His troops rallied and were sent hurtling into the Alps to face the Austrians.

The first battle commenced on April 12th, 1796, when French forces faced off against tens of thousands of Austrian soldiers. Napoleon was able to lead his troops to a soaring victory. Within a matter of moments, French artillery mowed down the Austrians. Thousands of Austrian troops perished in the first few rounds of fighting in the Battle of Montenotte. This battle would leave thousands of Austrians dead, and eventually, the Austrian forces were forced to make a hasty retreat.

It would take about a month of continued sustained losses, but the Austrians ultimately were driven out of Piedmont. It was a stunning success, and Napoleon was not afraid to boast of his achievement. After the Austrians were driven out, he declared, "Soldiers! In fifteen days, you have gained six victories, taken twenty-one colors and 55 pieces of artillery, seized several fortresses and conquered the richest parts of Piedmont."

And soon after, Napoleon would chase the Austrians all the way to Vienna. At this point, the Austrian emperor was forced to sue for peace. The subsequent peace talks led to the Treaty of Campo Formio.

This treaty was a great boon for France since it resulted in the French taking control of Piedmont and Lombardy (northern Italy). The French were also given control of the western bank of the Rhineland. However, it would not be long before France's foes would recalibrate and form a new coalition.

Chapter 8: The War of the Second Coalition and the Rise of Napoleon

"The battlefield is a scene of constant chaos. The winner will be the one who controls that chaos, both his own and the enemies."

-Napoleon Bonaparte

After Austria made peace with France, Britain had to fight the French alone. Nevertheless, the Austrians and the French continued to have issues with each other. There were still arguments over territorial disputes, and Austria was concerned about continued French warfare in other regions. In the summer of 1798, the French launched a sudden invasion of Egypt and Syria.

Napoleon shocked the world with this feat, as it seemed to come entirely out of left field. However, the move actually made a lot of sense. The French were not in a position to invade Britain as they would have liked due to insufficient naval strength to launch a cross-Channel invasion. But much of Britain's wealth at this time was due to its territorial possessions and trade networks that had been established through Egypt and onward all the way to India. In other words, the French were on a mission to cut off this valuable supply route.

Before getting to the coasts of North Africa, Napoleon Bonaparte's forces would make a pitstop at the island of Malta. Here, the French forces besieged an order of knights known as the Hospitallers. The

Hospitallers, who had their origins in the Crusades, had spent the past few centuries fending off Islamic incursions. Yet Napoleon was able to do what previous invading armies could not—he successfully laid siege to and overran the knights' fortifications. After just one day of fighting, the knights raised the white flag and handed over the island to Napoleon Bonaparte. The French now had the perfect weigh station to use on their way to Egypt.

The French ousting of the Hospitallers managed to incur the wrath of Russian Tsar Paul I. The Russian tsar had close ties with the knights and had been made an honorary "protector of the order" just prior to Napoleon's takeover of Malta. However, Russia was not about to declare war on France; instead, it sat on the sidelines to see how things would play out.

Egypt has shifted hands multiple times over the millennia. Of course, Egypt was the land of the pharaohs, who commissioned the building of the pyramids. The pharaohs were toppled by the armies of Alexander the Great. Egypt was made part of a Greek empire before it was seized by Rome, where it spent several centuries as the bread basket of the Roman Republic and then the Roman Empire. The Romans lost Egypt when Islamic armies swept down into the Middle East and North Africa.

The language of Egypt became Arabic, and its religion became Islam. Egypt would be administered by a wide range of Islamic dynasties, with one of those later dynasties being the Ottoman Empire. By the time of Napoleon's invasion, the Ottomans were in decline, and their grip on Egypt was weak. Egypt was essentially autonomous, being run by an Egyptian/Arabic group called the Mamluks.

Napoleon knew this. Part of his scheme was to defeat the Mamluks and then hand Egypt back to the Ottomans to curry the favor of the sultan. However, his plan had a fatal flaw since the sultan in faraway Turkey did not see the situation the same way Napoleon did. The Ottomans still considered Egypt theirs, and as soon as Napoleon and his troops landed, their actions were considered an act of war.

The French forces arrived in Egypt on June 30th, 1798. The landing was fraught with challenges. Napoleon had thousands of troops on foreign soil attempting to maneuver heavy artillery equipment in uncertain conditions. It certainly was not an easy task, but Napoleon was a man who liked a challenge. Napoleon and his army struggled onward and managed to reach the gates of Alexandria on July 2nd.

After a struggle, they seized a fortress situated right along the city walls. Napoleon then had a translator compile a written statement, which was delivered to the citizens of the city. The statement read, "People of Egypt. I come to restore your rights, to punish the usurpers; I respect God, his prophet and the Quran more than did the Mamluks. We are the friends of all true Muslims."

But the Egyptians were not so easily convinced. They took one look at these foreigners and decided they were not the friendly "liberators" they were claiming to be. Thus, the Egyptians continued to resist the French advance. As the French attempted to enter the city, they found they would have to battle practically the whole populace.

However, the outdated muskets used by the city's defenders were no match for Napoleon's cutting-edge artillery, giving the French a decisive advantage. Napoleon's forces were able to slice right through a desperate cavalry charge with punishing rounds of artillery. Alexandria was soon Napoleon's.

Britain responded to Napoleon's actions too late, but it still had a trick up its sleeve. The French fleet had already been battered by the British; Napoleon had taken what was left of it to make the trip to Egypt. In his haste to get to Alexandria, he left the craft unprotected. The British took advantage of this, sending its navy to bombard the French fleet. The ships were completely destroyed. Napoleon and his army were now marooned in Egypt.

Napoleon knew there was no turning back, so he went on the offensive and charged into Cairo. On July 21st, he launched what became known as the Battle of the Pyramids.

During this battle, Napoleon and his army faced off against an Egyptian Mamluk commander named Murad Bey. This exchange ended up turning out much like the battle in Alexandria. The Mamluk army was decimated, and Napoleon marched into Cairo on July 24th, 1798.

As successful as Napoleon was, there was a strong coalition forming against him. In fact, it was the formation of a second coalition, and it would lead to the War of the Second Coalition.

The coalition that waged this war against France took some time to form. The first step was when Naples allied itself with Austria, with the two joining forces on May 19th, 1798. The next major step was when Russia allied itself with Naples on November 29th. Shortly thereafter, the Austrian chancellor Johann Amadeus von Thugut attempted to bring the Prussians on board, but his efforts ultimately came to nothing.

Austria and Britain were not able to achieve a formal alliance, but they would unofficially cooperate in what has been termed "ad hoc cooperation." As these official and unofficial alliances were coming together, the next major piece of the puzzle was put in place when the Russians allied themselves with the Ottoman Empire on December 23rd and then with the British on December 26th of that fateful year of 1798.

One of the first major engagements of the coalition forces occurred the following year, in the summer of 1799, when a British/Russian force fought its way into the Netherlands. They battled the French and the Dutch forces that had aligned with them. The British and Russian forces were forced to retreat from the Netherlands after they were stymied by French forces in the Battle of Castricum on October 6th, 1799. Ultimately, the French and Dutch positions were too formidable, and the British/Russian troops were forced to retreat.

In the meantime, Napoleon had left Egypt for Gaza, where he defeated a strategic garrison at the city el-Arish. The French battled their way up the coast to the heavily fortified city of Acre. However, this Middle Eastern fortress proved to be too formidable, and Napoleon ended up retreating to Egypt. He arrived just in time to greet a British/Turkish army, which disembarked on July 11th.

The Turks managed to take the city of Aboukir, but a retooled French army led by Napoleon charged right into their positions. Thanks to the use of heavy artillery, the French were able to decimate their opponents. After this latest victory, Napoleon left his subordinates to sort out the administration of Egypt while he returned to France that October. He returned to bear witness to the latest problems in the body politic of France.

Since the eruption of new wide-ranging hostilities, the Directory instituted a highly unpopular draft, which forced men between the ages of twenty and twenty-five to enlist. Draft resistance was quite common, and troops often frequently deserted after being called to service. Morale was even lower when it was realized that the troops that did decide to fight would not be properly equipped due to a lack of proper goods.

Many blamed the French government's inability to properly equip its troops on deep-seated corruption in the Directory. All of this discontent led to yet another spate of political upheaval on June 18th, 1799, as four of the five directors of the Directory were ousted. Their replacements were considered "conservatives" and "revisionists" who wished to roll back the French Revolution to restore the rights that had been promised back in 1789.

It is worth noting that although the rights promised in 1789, such as the right to free speech, were considered liberal back in the days of the Tennis Court Oath, France had been through so much revolutionary turmoil that these basic rights were considered conservative. Although it might be hard to grasp, it does make some sense. The radical tenants of Maximilian Robespierre, which had led to the Reign of Terror and ultimately the Thermidorian Reaction, seemed far more revolutionary than the rights promised back in 1789.

However, there were still those who wanted more. People felt that the rights enshrined in the French Constitution did not go far enough. A very vocal group of Neo-Jacobins insisted that the newer variations of the French Constitution should stand and harangued the conservatives as being nothing short of "oligarchs." Napoleon waltzed right into this fray, and the conservative faction, seeking military support, sought his martial strength to put down their rivals.

They might have sought his help, but Bonaparte ultimately overthrew the Directory and took power himself. Napoleon and his troops launched a coup on November 9th, 1799. Bonaparte ordered that the current constitution be discarded in favor of drafting a new one. Bonaparte was placed in a position to oversee all of these changes as the first consul. Although he was not yet calling himself emperor, the position of first consul essentially gave Napoleon final authority over all matters of governance. This coup is typically seen as the end of the French Revolution, as Napoleon would bring some stability to the country.

Napoleon continued to lead the troops. In early June, the French were able to seize Milan and then a whole string of towns, such as Pavia, Piacenza, Stradella, and other parts of the Lombardy region. This effectively cut off the Austrian supply lines heading east along the banks of the Po River. The French then collided with the Austrian army in the vicinity of Marengo on June 14th. The French numbered around twenty-eight thousand, while the Austrians were thirty thousand strong. Along with a numerical advantage, the Austrians also had better artillery.

But the fighting spirit was with the French, and they were able to completely drive the Austrians from Italy. This victory not only solidified French positions in Italy but also Napoleon Bonaparte's position in the

French government. The conquering hero Napoleon (at least for the moment) could do no wrong.

It was just a brief walk to outright absolutism, with Napoleon being made consul for life in 1802 and then the emperor of France in 1804. It was also declared that the imperial mantle would carry on as a hereditary title through Napoleon's offspring. Yes, after several years of terrible bloodshed in which the French monarchy had been overthrown, the French found themselves back at square one by instituting a new absolute monarchy.

Ever since the 1791 constitution, the French government had experimented with representative republicanism, which ultimately led to the Directory and its bicameral legislature. However, all of these efforts were stopped in their tracks when Napoleon took over. Until Napoleon was overthrown, all legislature would be executive in nature, and it would be enacted at the dictatorial whims of Napoleon Bonaparte.

Although Napoleon later became the emperor of France, it is very important to make note of the fact that Napoleon was a major promoter of the ideals of the Enlightenment. Yes, he was a despot, but he was an enlightened despot. Also, Napoleon Bonaparte stands out as a clear indication that history and its principal characters are far more complicated than we typically give them credit. Napoleon might have ruled with an iron fist, but he also ensured that many of the basic freedoms espoused by the great minds of the Enlightenment were put in place.

In a strange twist, Napoleon, a man whose own personal morality many might have questioned even then, had been placed as the gatekeeper of morality in France. He arrived when France was at a juncture between anarchy and chaos, and it was suddenly up to him to ensure that the basic personal freedoms gained by the French were not lost. So, he had to use the powers at his disposal to keep that from happening, even though those powers were more of an absolute monarch than a representative government.

Under Napoleon, a person was free (at least for the most part) in France, but that freedom had limits. People weren't free to randomly attack, rob, and brutalize those they did not like, but they were free to have their own basic rights as long as they did not interfere with others. And just like the former rights that were espoused by the Enlightenment, these freedoms only affected men, not women. Also, as time passed,

Napoleon reinstated slavery, which had been banned by the French government in 1795.

Still, in many ways, the basic freedoms that Napoleon enforced created the much-needed balance of basic liberties and a clear and stable legal framework. The Napoleonic Code outlined the people's freedoms while simultaneously ensuring that those freedoms would not get out of hand as they had during the French Revolution. The Napoleonic Code established clear and concise guidelines that could not be altered at the mere whim of passionate mobs, biased judges, or other unforeseen events.

In contrast to the shifting sands of the Reign of Terror, which had been brought on by the French Revolution and stirred up all manner of wild accusations, trumped-up charges, and mob rule, Napoleon's new legal framework would not be swayed by rumors and gossip. The Napoleonic Code was put in place as a solid bulwark upon which society could rest.

The Napoleonic Code was so stable that its legacy continues to be a major part of French society to this very day. So, yes, Napoleon was a dictator and caused all kinds of war and turmoil in multiple countries during the course of his many military adventures. But we also must give credit where credit is due. And we must acknowledge the legal stability that was established during Napoleon Bonaparte's time in power.

Conclusion: The Lasting Impact of the French Revolution

The French Revolution was an impactful event in France and world history. Although the French Revolution was sparked to answer a major dilemma facing the French people, its ramifications ended up affecting the whole world.

Much has been said about how many of the ideals and actions of the French Revolution inspired other global movements, but let's take a look at a movement that often gets overlooked in favor of the Latin American independence wars, for example. Karl Marx was inspired by the French commune of Paris.

The notion that the common man of the street could shake off an entrenched power like the French monarchy has left a lasting legacy. And those who wished to do likewise in other parts of the world would look toward the French Revolution as both an example and an inspiration.

Despite all of the bloodshed, terror, and repercussions, the French Revolution stood out as some sort of beacon of hope. After all, the French Revolution overturned the normal state of affairs and allowed the common person to voice their grievances. It was only in the later stages of the revolution that this spirit was lost, as the Jacobins and others among the revolutionary elite wished to crack down and solidify their gains. This tyrannical maneuver has been widely repeated by oppressive tyrants and regimes that have come on the heels of bloody revolutions.

Lenin and Stalin promised the same kind of utopian freedoms to their people as the French did. And just like Robespierre at his worst, they decided to dispatch with the revolutionaries once they had served their purpose.

The intellectual elites felt they knew how to fashion society better than anyone else. They were seeking to recreate civilization (and even spirituality) in their own image. Nothing captures the height of this hubris than Robespierre's "cult of the Supreme Being." Even his colleagues could not help but balk at these shenanigans. And if he had not been stopped, it is quite possible that he might have achieved his aim of creating a religion with himself as its head.

The executions and persecution during the French Revolution, something that were seen as "civil" solutions to social problems at the time, would be latched onto and repeated by the most despicable political movements. The French chose to kill enemies of the state by way of guillotine because they viewed this instrument as a humane way to fix the social ills that plagued France.

This was the same sentiment expressed by the Nazis, who opted to create elaborate gas chambers to kill those whom they deemed "undesirable." Nazi bureaucrats, such as Joseph Goebbels and Heinrich Himmler, were notorious paper pushers who recoiled at the mere sight of blood, yet they were okay with authorizing the deaths of millions by way of gas.

In much the same way, the French revolutionaries felt the guillotine was a humane way to kill others. This belief was actually professed by this instrument of the Reign of Terror's namesake, Dr. Joseph-Ignace Guillotin. He declared that this device of death, which ultimately took his own name, the guillotine, was the best means to ensure his own "philanthropic" sense of humanitarianism.

To be fair to Dr. Guillotin, he most certainly never dreamed that this instrument of death would be used for large-scale indiscriminate killing. Guillotin was more likely envisioning this tool of execution to be the last resort and used to execute condemned criminals in a humane way. Before the guillotine, people were subjected to horrendous torture and cruel deaths. For instance, the breaking wheel was a popular form of public execution. A criminal would be tied to the floor and then have his bones broken by way of this large, heavy wheel, which sometimes had spikes on it. The wheel would be dropped on the body again and again, crushing the bones of its victims. Next, the criminal would be strapped to the wheel and placed on a pole. The executioner would then decapitate or strangle the accused to death. Sometimes, a criminal would be strapped to the wheel and thrown into a fire. Even a typical beheading, a form of execution that was reserved for the nobility, often took more than one try to decapitate the accused, leading to cries of agony instead of a swift death.

The breaking wheel would be abolished in 1791, but it was just one of many excruciating punishments from this time. In light of this, it makes sense that men like Guillotin sought a humane way to get rid of criminals who could not be reformed. Guillotin actually sought to end capital punishment, but he was not successful. So, he instead sought a means to humanely put those guilty of murder, brutal assault, and the most heinous of crimes to death. Dr. Guillotin likely did not foresee the guillotine being used to silence political opposition on a massive scale.

Unlike Guillotin, the French revolutionaries who readily employed the guillotine did not hesitate to use the guillotine as their means of crushing their opponents. They believed that with the quick pull of a cord and the hissing of a blade, political opponents could be silenced quickly without much effort or having to hear their cries for very long. The killing was easy. Today, we would liken it to pushing a button to get rid of someone. The ease with which people were killed via the guillotine helped to desensitize the executioners and those ordering the executions.

After the fall of Robespierre, Napoleon Bonaparte came along and brought some sanity back to French society. It is true that he was a military dictator, but he did bring back a sense of normalcy with his Napoleonic Code. He also restored the church. Although Napoleon was not particularly devout, he probably figured that if people needed religion, they might as well keep the one they were familiar with instead of creating a brand new one.

Napoleon would ultimately be deposed, and the French would face more problems. There was a brief return to the constitutional monarchy until the rise of Napoleon III, the nephew of the original imperial upstart. It was only after the fall of Napoleon III that France took on its more familiar shape of a modern-day republic, with senators and a sitting president at its head.

France has been through quite a few twists and turns in history, and the whole world has been affected as a consequence. To this very day, the French Revolution still stands as one of the starkest examples of both the best and worst of humanity. The French Revolution brought us the Rights of Man and of the Citizen but also the "terror" of the guillotine. Great intellectual thought and discourse were matched by the unreasoning belligerence of mobs. The French Revolution was a perplexing paradox that both intrigues and haunts us to this very day.

Here's another book by Enthralling History that you might like

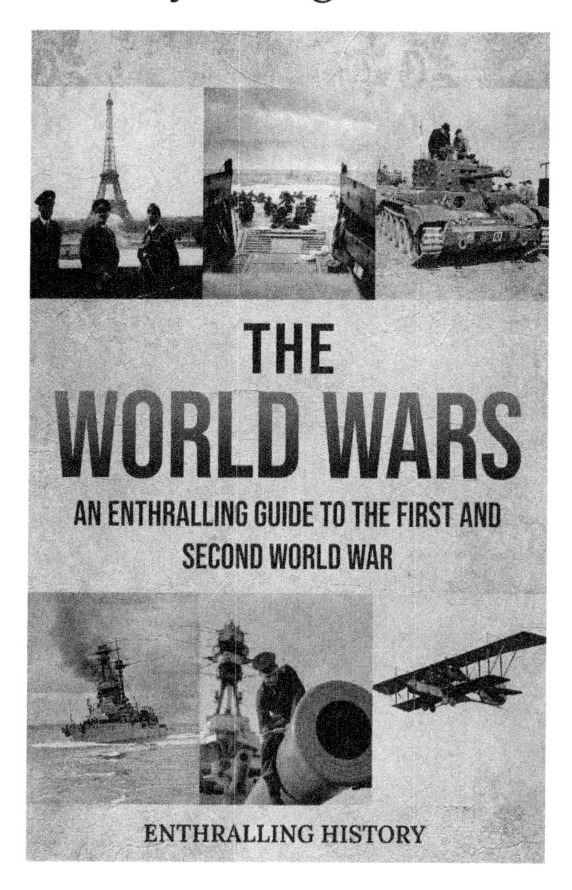

Free limited time bonus

Stop for a moment. We have a free bonus set up for you. The problem is this: we forget 90% of everything that we read after 7 days. Crazy fact, right? Here's the solution: we've created a printable, 1-page pdf summary for this book that you're reading now. All you have to do to get your free pdf summary is to go to the following website:

https://livetolearn.lpages.co/enthrallinghistory/

Once you do, it will be intuitive. Enjoy, and thank you!

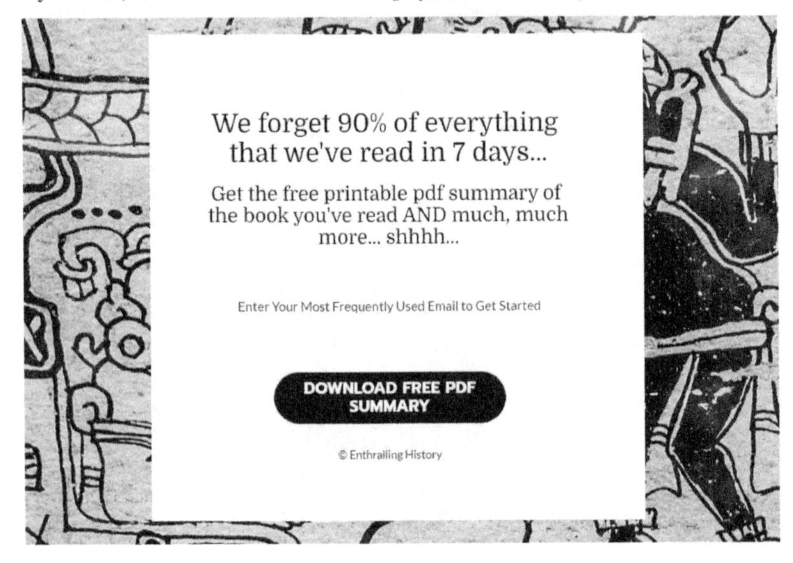

Appendix A: Further Reading and References

Alexander, Martin S. *French History Since Napoleon.* 1999.

Haine, W. Scott. *The History of France.* 2000.

Popkin, Jeremy D. *A History of Modern France.* 1994.

Price, Roger. *A Concise History of France.* 2005.

Harper, Rob. *Fighting the French Revolution: The Great Vendée Rising.* 2019.

Hibbert, Christopher. *The Days of the French Revolution.* 1980.

Klar, Jeremy. *The French Revolution, Napoleon, and the Republic.* 2015.

Salvemini, Gaetano. *The French Revolution: 1788-1792.* 1954.

Schama, Simon. *Citizens: A Chronicle of the French Revolution.* 1989.

Yonge, Charles. *The Life of Marie Antoinette.* 1876